Clinging to the Cross...

... between the Stones and the Firelight:

Book 1

Mark Tanner

LITTLE HOUSE IN
- JOPPA -

Little House in Joppa Publishing
Abbey Street, Chester, CH1 2JD, UK

admin@little-house-in-joppa.uk

First edition: 2023

ISBN: 978-1-7392688-0-0

DEDICATION

---

*For the people of the Diocese of Chester:
those I know personally and all I am yet to meet
but am still privileged to serve as your bishop.*

INDEX

PREFACE TO THE FIRST EDITION

It is a number of years since I started writing the material which has become this series. I wrote to help me think and pray through my increasing uneasiness at the impasse we appeared to be reaching about questions of sexuality in the church and realised I was wrestling with all sorts of other complex questions at the same time. Jesus seemed to be able to cut through all manner of tangles when he faced them, but we keep coming up against red-lines, hard walls, and broken relationships. How do we 'do' faithfulness in complexity? How do we do kindness and clarity in a Christlike way?

Meeting Jesus changes everything for all who meet him. Here we search the scriptures to explore how we can meet Christ afresh in a world where questions seem to get bigger and opinions stronger with every passing year. It is so easy to hear only the loudest voices, but Christ is calling his people.

As the Church of England's *Living in Love and Faith* (LLF) project comes to a conclusion, I realise it might be helpful these reflections to offer to the Diocese of Chester which I serve here in the North West of England. It engages with many issues, and the ground covered by LLF is part of what it considers. Publishing timings don't normally allow for this speed of delivery, but I can offer this slightly more rough and ready, less edited version, and thus do so with humility. (The material is, of course, available to anyone, though: you are welcome whoever you are as you read, and I pray you will meet with Christ as you do.)

Please forgive typos (you are welcome to point them out if you wish, sending them to corrections@little-house-in-joppa.uk with book title, format, and page number), and please remember that this is thinking which is still in process for me as well as for you.

You will find questions for reflection at the end of each of the main chapters. This is, partly, because groups might like to use this material as study material. It also, though, helps readers engage with this material as devotional.

My prayer is that, in reading this and wrestling with the various topics we explore you will find your faith deepened, your understanding enlarged, and your heart warmed.

God bless you as you enter this space which we shall come to know as the space between the Stones and the Firelight.

† Mark
December 2022

PROLOGUE

———————————

You might like to listen to this before reading on
(it was designed to be heard more than read),
but it's up to you.

It's a fresh day, yet here we are again: bright hope of a new dawn marred by the behaviour of the woman in front of us. She knows it's wrong, I know it's wrong, there is nothing to question... but I would still rather be anywhere but here. Oh, don't get me wrong; the Bible is clear and I know what needs to be done. Keep this kind of behaviour at a distance! It is a slippery slope and letting standards slide in one matter only leads to the destruction of the whole. Think of Sodom and Gomorrah. Look at the nations round us. God's judgement is clear. Don't let us be polluted, tainted, by the likes of her.

And so we gather. Righteous. Angry. Certain.

Teacher, we say, what do you say we should do? We caught this woman in the very act, and the law is clear She deserves to die.

I can't help feeling we have interrupted something. A conversation?

I wish I had been here before.

I wish he would say something.

What's he fiddling around in the sand for?

We are ready; stones in hand. The only contact I want with this woman is to hurl my condemnation and go. Go and weep. Over her? Over our world? Suddenly I am not so sure.

What I do know for sure is that there is an unbridgeable chasm between the likes of me and the likes of her. I obey the word. She obviously doesn't. I am holy. She isn't. I guess, as I look at him, that I kind of regret that there is no other way to reach across as I suddenly realise how close I am standing... how his gaze catches us both without even moving his head. But why am I even thinking that? The Scriptures are clear, and there can be no other way. Her death will deter others. An eye for an eye. Judgement stands as its own warning.

And finally! he speaks.

What's that?

Oh! That's OK then!

Oh!

Oh?

And as the stone slips from my fingers... as it thuds into the dirt by my feet... as I feel those feet move unbidden and I slip away into the brightening day, I am not sure where I am headed now. Might I hear more? How can such a sentence be changed with just a sentence? Who is this man, after all? How do I know which way ahead?

It's a new day, and I am so glad I dropped my stone.

Note about the reflections...

... which, in some ways, could do with being read before the first one, except that I am in a bind. I want the impact of the Scriptures to be the primary point of encounter in these books. I want this both in the sense of it being the first thing that you come across, dear reader, and the main thing that shapes our thinking. However, there are two things that you need to know.

Firstly, and most importantly: this series is shaped by the Bible but not in the sense that I have decided that the Bible says a particular thing and this is an argument to support that thing. The older I get, the more I am convinced that the Bible is a book to be heard in company at least as much as it is a book to be read alone. I know I am setting up an overly-heightened dichotomy here, for the sake of making the point, but there are important potential differences, including:

- Hearing words does not happen alone; there are at least two people involved in an act of hearing, and usually more (even if one of them is recorded, they are still 'other' to the hearer). The Bible is a collection of books written for communities spanning many contexts and times, and in faith we receive it as such.
  Reading tends to be individual, which is very fitting to our culture but is problematic if our reception of a text blinds us to the intention of the author.
- Hearing, therefore, includes encounter (at the very least with one other). It is of the heart as well as of the mind.
  Reading can, but needn't, include interaction with any other, other than the text.
- Hearing provokes imagination and invites retelling. It invites us into a shared experience, conversation, story, and community.
  Reading can do the same, but it can also draw us into isolated study and development of particular individual viewpoints and arguments.

- Hearing offers opportunity for discussion and shared development of ideas. I think this is true even if you don't talk with others as you listen: for example, if you are offended by something but no one else is that shapes the way you respond. Similarly, if you laugh when others don't, or the level of energy either in the speaker or in the room rises. We are social beings and we are informed and shaped as people by this shared engagement.
  Reading alone can and does do this to some extent, but is far less rich and can lead to development of individual ideas and arguments in isolation from others and the wider world.

Hearing, in other words, actively allows others to invite you to inhabit a shared space that is infinitely more wonderful and varied than any one participant in that place will grasp by themselves. Reading can be participative in the same way, but needs to be allowed to do so. This is what I want the books in this series to do: to invite you afresh into a space with Christ where it is not so much that you leave knowing more, but leave knowing him more; not so much that you are given knowledge, but leave having tasted wisdom (God's not mine!); not so much that you have been persuaded, more that you have been wooed afresh by the God who calls you to life and grace in his Son.

Secondly, I do not know how well any of these reflections work written down. They, too, were written to be spoken aloud because I am far more of a preacher than I am a writer. When talking to a group a practiced speaker can respond to the feedback they receive in all manner of unconscious ways, but I cannot do that in the same way when writing. I am happy to share the text, but I have also recorded the reflections in order that you can inhabit the space they are intended to create before each section of the book.

You will see both a QR code (the blobby black square) and a web address at the top of each one. If you point your smartphone or tablet's camera at the QR code or type the address into a device connected to the internet it should take you to the recording.

Please allow these reflections to invite you into the presence of Christ. I have written each as a stand-alone piece, but positioned them to open up our thinking/praying/reflecting on each section and to try enable us to be shaped by the Scriptures. Do listen and try to listen with your head, your heart, and your soul, but also pause and dwell for a moment in the text. This is an ancient way of reading the Bible with some of the work done for you. St Ignatius of Loyola set out ways of doing 'Lectio Divina' (Godly reading) which help us inhabit the biblical text, although the practice of Lectio is based on the ways Jews read the Scriptures at Passover and has been part of Christian practice since St Gregory of Nyssa taught about it in the 4th Century. These reflections are simply some of my written lectios offered to you. Your own reading will be just as valid, possibly even more so. May mine, though, be a springboard into each section of this book and its companion volumes, an invitation and a spur into further engagement.

INTRODUCTION

_____

This may well not be the book you want it to be, but it might just be the book you need it to be, at least in small part.

It is also not the complete book, but rather the first of three that sit together. Together they do not so much offer you a fish as provide a fishing manual, to borrow an image[1].

I am not setting out to tell you what do to, but rather to explore how we live well and wisely as we consider what to do in following Christ. I used to teach trainee ministers ('ordinands' as we call them in the Church of England), and one of the first things I would say to them was that they had come to be trained to serve a world that had not yet come into being, as part of a church which we had not yet imagined, with a gospel that was relevant to all in every season. My task now, as it was then, is to try to offer insight into the skills of faithful improvisation around the unchanging melody of the gospel set in the constantly evolving drama of everyday life. If you are wrestling with something specific this might seem frustrating at first, but please persevere! Possibly (but only possibly) I could plate up a ready-made answer for you, but in so doing I would not prepare you for the next thing you face, and I would rob the world of the wisdom you will develop and share. These practices are well worth the price.

_____

[1] There is, I believe, an old Chinese proverb that says 'Give a man a fish and he will eat for a day, teach him to fish and he will eat for a lifetime.'

Here we are searching for wisdom, not merely answers.

This and the two books that follow in *the Stones and the Firelight* series are books about sexuality, but only a little bit about sexuality. They springboard from questions that arise in our seemingly interminable conversations about sex and asks what God is teaching us about faithful living that might draw us forward in grace, liberty, and life. One of the things that I wonder if God might be doing through our various debates in this area (and I am in no doubt that God will be doing many different things through them given that he is good, loving, and able) is to open bigger questions of discipleship. Honestly, though, I would prefer to start somewhere else, if I could, not least because most people I bump into don't really appear to want to know what others think about sex, gender, or identity unless they either agree with them or can use their views as something to kick against. They may want to talk but few want to listen about it. I guess that this is fair enough given the amount we hear others talk on the subject, and it is no surprise that most of us want affirmation, assurance, acceptance, and support. We want people to agree with us, affirm our perspective, and offer arguments in support of the views that we either have or would like to have; this area of life is no different but it does sometimes feel more pointed.

In truth, I don't know that I have anything new to say about sexuality.

Perhaps more worryingly than my suspicion I have nothing new to say on that topic, I don't know if I would be willing to say it even if I did have, and I say this for two reasons. Negatively, as we will discuss at the start of books 2 and 3, responsibility for both for words and the way that we use emotions is multifaceted and we are very effective at shutting others down in this area. I notice two responses to this: to shout or to shut-up. I don't like shouting, which is, perhaps, why the first draft of this text has sat on my (digital) shelf for well over three years. More positively, I realise I don't want to put a book in your hand that prolongs argument or reinforces a tribal position. I want to give you a gift that will help you look to Christ and follow humbly, wisely, and with increasing confidence. This is what I have set out to write. I will describe my journey into this reflection in an appendix (from page 112) as this might be of interest, however I put it at the end because it is not the main point of the book.

I offer what follows here and in the subsequent books very cautiously, with humility and a significant degree of nervousness. I will not be right in everything I say, and even what I do get right I could probably have said better. It seems difficult to talk about some of the things we will touch on without appearing to either lecture or judge others, and ending up hurting them, estranging them, or making them angry in the process. I don't want to do any of that (deliberately or accidentally). However, the more I reflect, the more I realise that the questions I am pondering are not really about sex, sexuality, gender identity, or other big issues that face us. These questions matter, but it is also helpful to notice that they are today's way into thinking about bigger questions. Such questions have always been part of following Christ, albeit that our specific areas of debate will feel new because every generation tends to think that it faces things which no-one can possibly have faced before.

The more I listen, the more it seems to me that people are struggling with exactly the question that I am wrestling with. How do I live in a way that is faithful to Christ, formed by the Scriptures, and loving to those around me? How do I follow well in a world (and sometimes a church) that so often seems at odds with my faith? And how do I do this in a way which is shared and not simply about me, my righteousness, or my own peace of mind?

The more I reflect, the more I realise that just as this is not about any one issue, neither is it a question just for me. The real question of our age (perhaps of every age) is something like: how do we 'do' faithfulness? How do we live well between the stones (of the opening reflection in each book) and the firelight (that we will be invited to see afresh at the close of each text) in the light of which the church and the rock on which we are built would be shaped for all eternity.

Note the structure of the book(s)...

... and choose where to start!

Before I dive into some health warnings that we might want to bear in mind as we engage in this material, let me point out the obvious truth that books do not have to be read in the set order from beginning to end. This arrangement is the one that makes best sense to me, but you might be better served by reading in a different order. This is always true, but particularly when you are dealing with an extended thought worked out under three separate sections (which became three books late in the writing and publishing process).

In each of the three books (on the themes of cross, exile, and powerlessness) you will find the same shaping so that material revolves around five chapters:

- A reflection
- Some exploration and explanation of the theme of the book
- Potentially problematic ways in which we might receive that theme
- Insights or lessons that we might wish to note
- A reflection on one way we might choose to live in response to this theme and our emerging thinking.

In between each chapter there will be a brief pausing for breath to help us reflect. These simple questions are intended to draw your mind and heart back to your own engagement with the issues that you face. Please use them as you wish. Please read as you would like to: each person who reads this is different, with different experience, needs, questions, and preferences. My only real plea is that you don't skip the bible material.

In the rest of this chapter you will find:

- Pages 11-17: Health and Safety alerts for diligent readers – some things to note which might help you as you read.
- Pages 17-20: Overview and Prayer – sketching the shape of the book and praying for you as you read it.

In addition, this book ends with an appendix, as described above, offering three bits of background to the material as I first wrestled with it:

- Pages 112-122: A personal introduction – a snapshot of the journey I have taken to get to these books.
- Pages 122-120: An ecclesiological (churchy) introduction – looking at where the Church (of England, at least) is at the moment.
- Pages 120-127: A (Western) cultural introduction – stepping back and briefly considering the broader context in which I write.

I describe all this with the hope that I can enable and encourage you to be reflective in your engagement. I hope that you will be pondering in reading just as I am pondering in writing. Please don't assume that you will suddenly come to a clear thought or feeling which will immediately be persuasive to everyone else. As I have said, this is not a book intended to win arguments: it is, rather, one to help you reflect deeply and live wisely. We live, and we are called to live, in a very complicated world.

Health and Safety alerts for diligent readers

I kicked off this chapter by expressing the thought that this is probably not the book that you would like it to be. I suspect that this is true on many levels and is not merely defensive self-deprecation. We will be pondering challenging areas of life and doing so in a way which invites change (because we will set out to explore scripture, invite prayer, consider others, and meet the living God... not because I will try to demand change of you).

In treading this ground, both in our reading and any conversation we have arising from this area of reflection, it seems to me that there are various cautions we would be wise to bear in mind. More precisely, let me share the five cautions I have in mind as I wield the tools in this workshop: you can do your own risk assessment for your context.

Power

Firstly, I need to attend to issues of power; both power that I may or may not hold, and the power that you hold over me (whether or not you see or feel it).

Most of the time when I speak I am doing so in a context where I have a captive audience and I occupy the privileged position of speaker and (usually) of bishop. In some ways it is not the same with writing: I have no idea you are reading this, and you can easily put down this book. However, we often have an inbuilt bias that suspects that something in a book is probably more right than something found on the internet or heard down the pub. Someone has chosen to write this and publish it, after all. (Incidentally, at least in my experience, it doesn't usually feel like I am exercising power when I speak or write, but this just makes it even more important that I am aware that I do.) When an author writes or a minister speaks in public for the sake of Christ and his Kingdom, they are there to minister to the flock in front of them rather than to further their own agenda or promote a particular personal cause. This is complex and tangled, of course, but it is always wise to attend to issues of power, and this is especially true when it comes to questions that speak deeply into matters of human identity and around which hearers may well already be feeling vulnerable.

Thus, I fool myself if I believe I can or should write only for myself. I am not the most important person in this conversation: you matter. How will you read this book if you are [and here I insert the names, the faces, the situations, the sound of the voices of many people I have spoken with over the years]? I (probably) don't know you, but I have a responsibility towards you and I wish to exercise it well. More than this, I apologise in advance where I get this wrong.

You, also, have power in this conversation, even though it probably does not feel like it. You have power with regard to me: I do not wish to hurt, anger, or inconvenience you. I do want to offer something you choose to read. In writing with an imagined you in mind, I shape my tone and content and I need to be aware of this if I am to pursue wisdom. You also have tremendous power when it comes to living in the light of these conversations. We will return to this in the last of these three books which addresses powerlessness. For now, we merely note that it is a dynamic of which we must be aware.

Thinking out loud

Secondly, I am not sure that it is always responsible to think 'out loud', although I fear that even this sentence will not be heard for what it is intended to say. This is a piece of cake that we want both to have and to eat. When something complex matters to us, we often want someone to process it with and depending on our personality type it may or may not be clear that we are working something out. It is good to know that someone is listening to our views and thinking about them with us. However, we are not always as nuanced when it comes to their views. We can assume that anything others say on an issue is their settled position on the matter, and define them by what they have said without really pausing to check if they are thinking out loud. The world is a simpler place when it is split into 'goodies' and 'baddies'.

Sometimes I wonder if many of the problems we have in the church in this area stem from the church failing to grasp how the modern world communicates and its obsession with scandal. We, the church, talk in a way which is meant to be exploratory but is heard as communicating something definite.

We mean one thing, but are heard saying something else. Historically the Church of England, for example, has been one of the safest places in the UK for LGBTQI+ people, but you would never know that if based on today's media or social media[2]. Quick speech on this issue, whether in private conversation or public address, seems to lead either into argument or into an echo chamber and neither is helpful for developing thought or wisdom. This is true for everyone, but I note it particularly for those of us with a responsibility to teach and preserve the faith. Teachers are judged strictly, as James points out[3], and the dangers around this area are manifold: we are dealing with people's lives at a profound level. Immediate answers might be popular, but wisdom takes time to grow, and we need to take care not to speak for the sake of speaking. I am not claiming I will get to wisdom in this search, but I do know that I definitely won't get there simply by shouting above the bustle of the modern marketplace.

Communicating Complexity

Thirdly, I observe that we, as a society, have a communication problem both when we are in broadcast mode and when we are in receive mode when we talk about deep stuff. When we talk, we fall easily into pre-cast patterns of language without questioning how they are heard, and when we listen we often think that we know what people are going to say and fail to notice that they are trying to communicate something different. Without getting all culturally elitist, it is true to say that this is exacerbated by the entertainment we consume, which I enjoy just as much as the next person. Watch pretty

---

[2] I would argue that this has been true in practice as the church has been a place where people unsure about their own sexuality (or sure, but equally sure they will not be accepted) have found security over the years. It has also been true in terms of action. The Church of England was a leading partner in decriminalising homosexuality in the UK, not because there was any desire to change doctrine per se, but because of a respect for the person and a belief that this was not criminal activity.

[3] See James 3.1

much anything on your favourite streaming platform and part of the easy joy is that you know where the story is going long before it gets there. You can drop in an out of the story, double-screening, engaging in conversation, and popping out to check on tea... all of this is fine because the medium and content on screen is designed to be easy to follow and draw you into the drama. Even if you miss something you can 'rewind' and work it out. This is popular because it is easy, and it is in step with instant communication, pre-packaged advertising, and carefully spun 'party-lines'. The trouble is that real conversations are much harder work. When you talk with an equal who is not trying to sell you something, both hearer and speaker have a responsibility for communication, and such responsibility is only worked out if both take it seriously. If I assume I know what you are going to say, I will not hear you. Equally, when I just broadcast my views without working to understand what you are hearing, I cannot be surprised when you 'misunderstand'.

(We shall return to this in the introduction to Book 2)

Understanding

Fourthly, and more specifically, never mind that we need to work at understanding each other: I am really struck by the fact that sometimes we seem to struggle even to try to listen to each other in areas of disagreement (like sexuality); and sadly, this is true within the church as well as without. One of the things that stalled the first draft of this text a few years ago was (separately) meeting two good friends whom I don't actually see all that often. We happened to meet just as I came to the end of my scribbling. Both asked me what I was up to at the moment, which was kind and natural, but what was really striking was the change that came upon them when I mentioned the area I was pondering. Each of them dived straight into their own thoughts around faith and human sexuality before I had drawn breath, even though this was not really what I was pondering. In one case the conversation just took a whole new, and quite interesting turn. In the other it took an uncomfortable defensive direction I had not foreseen as my normally non-judgmental friend assumed all manner of assertions that I must be making.

Both conversations were interesting in their own way, and I receive each as gift; it is a privilege to listen. They were an interesting object lesson, too, though, and there are a number of explanations for this unusual behaviour. It could be that my friends wanted to correct my thinking or approach concerning such issues, although I note that neither took the time to establish what I thought before they launched into their views, and it is ironic that the questions they discussed were not my focus anyway. This would, probably accurately, bely the deep sense of conviction that most people seem hold on this issue (although the convictions differ). It could be that they feel that the issue is sorted, although the two of them said quite different things to each other. I might just be being late to the party though. Or, and this makes me ponder, is there an element of truth in the thought that most of us feel that we cannot really explore complex questions with others so it whirrs in our heads until someone invites us to think about it? How far is our behaviour determined by this being a repressed question?

Fear

Finally, arising from these: when I look with care I note that there is fear associated with speaking in this area. I dare to name it in myself but I see it in others too. I fear hurting pople. I fear turning folk away from Christ. And on a less important, but no less real level, I fear being judged. I don't have any confidence that my wrestling will be heard for what it is. It's amazing how easy it is to be hated by both sides of an argument: in this case to be both despised because I need to be honest and say that revisionist readings of the Scriptures do not seem to me to engage with the whole of the Scriptures in a robust and defensible way, and simultaneously loathed because I am not sure that this is the main point that the Bible itself would want us to be focussing on. What does this matter, you may well ask? I am a privileged, white, able-bodied, straight bloke who has plenty of influence already, and any fears I may have pale into insignificance before the torments others face in this area. This is probably true, and shapes me into someone who is far more inclined to listen than to speak, but it is also something I need to note because it will inevitably inhibit Godly thinking and the search for wisdom. Fear is not a context which is conducive to faith, which is why it is driven out by love[4], and why we need to care for each other in this discussion. We are all dealing with deep issues of theology, identity, belonging, love, and faith.

Overview of the Series

In my wrestling, then, I find that I am engaging with three big biblical themes and seeing where they lead me. I am not trying to 'answer the sexuality question' (or any other one specific question), whatever that would mean. I am trying to consider how we live faithfully, and reflect on three massive motifs I find scrawled through pretty much every page of the Bible but rarely (if ever, when it comes to the second and third of them) hear preached about. I don't claim any great authoritative source or divine revelation; this is simply my own prayer, reflection, and pondering as I read my Bible and pray for those around me.

The issue I bump into is that the priorities that I read about in my morning devotions are very commonly different to the ones I see reflected around me in the wider world, and concerningly frequently different to the ones I hear discussed in the church (at least by me, don't let me thrust the responsibility for this on others). So, for example, the Bible is basically the story of repeated exile (from Eden, into Egypt, into Babylon, and so on),

---

[4] See 1 John 4.18 and the context of that passage.

but I can't think of the last time this was mentioned in a sermon I have heard or of anyone wrestling with the question of exile in the new covenant of Christ (despite the language of the book of Peter, for example). It has long seemed to me that this is a missing narrative in our self understanding as Christians, and we need to explore it if we are to make sense of the present and enable participation in the body of Christ. There is so much in the Bible about exile, and we don't really reflect on it in a Christian context beyond Sunday-School level insights about the naughty people of Israel. Perhaps it is unfair, but I am not sure relegating our understanding of exilic themes to the divine equivalent of a naughty-step really does sufficient justice to a major strand of biblical teaching.

We need to engage with the questions raised by exile under the new covenant, and I think we will be surprised at what we begin to glimpse. Book 2 addresses this theme.

The same is true, only rather more shockingly vivid in its contrast, about power. The Bible is full of caution about power, but we frequently seem to seek and embrace it. Whether we look at the kings portrayed in the Hebrew Scriptures or the pattern of Jesus' teaching, surely this is problematic. Perhaps I feel this with particular poignancy given the strange position I am called to occupy (and I do believe that it is a call), but we get comfortable with power at our own peril. We cannot (usually) walk away from the responsibilities with which we are entrusted, but neither can we lightly assume that they are ours by right. I am a steward, a servant, a child; these things belong together by the choice of the one who invites and calls.

Book 3 wrestles with this question of how we engage well with power.

And this book, in particular:

The key, and thus the first, area of reflection to which I keep returning, though, is around the cross. I hope I would do so anyway, but I am concerned never to stop thinking about the cross: I reference it often, but find myself falling back on formulaic explanations when I talk about it. I am not sure that this is good enough. In my own prayers, I find myself repeatedly exploring what God was and is doing as he engages with our broken world, and it is this cruciform[5] thinking that has provoked the need to tidy up my head by setting it out on paper. Above all we must grasp the cross if we are to be faithful to the crucified saviour; we will never fully understand every dynamic at work on Calvary, but this is where worship, salvation, ethics, and Christian identity is rooted. We need to glimpse afresh each day what it is that we are invited into, both as recipients *of*, and as participants *in* God's grace.

So, these books are shaped around reflections on the question of powerlessness (book 3), the importance of exile (book 2), and the call to crucifixion (in the pages that follow here). As I have mentioned, in each you will find a similar pattern:

- A reflection, a kind of devotional meditation on a passage of the Bible. This is, if you like such terms, basically a written lectio: an imaginative resting in the text to try to live it as well as understand it. I want to be shaped by the Scriptures not merely educated by them, nourished by them more than merely being urged on by them, and held by them rather than simply holding them.
- An exploration of the biblical theme, which is a snapshot of work in progress rather than the finished article.
- Some reflections on lessons I am learning from the theme in practical life.
- Some ponderings around common mistakes it seems to me that we can make if we don't take this theme seriously.
- And finally, a few musings on what God may be calling us into in terms of our shared lives of discipleship.

None of this, of course, will be exhaustive. Neither my inner capacity nor the space and time I have for this work would allow me to set myself so high a bar and, thus, to me every chapter

---

[5] Or cross-shaped: I use 'cruciform' as it reminds me that I am talking specifically about the cross of Christ.

still feels not-quite-finished. The perfectionist in me rails against this, but the realist points out this will always be the case, and the pragmatist notes that each of us needs to absorb and advance the thinking for ourselves anyway. My hope in writing is that it will start an interesting and valuable conversation on what it means to love one another in Christ, what it means to participate in his mission, and how we lift our hearts in worship when we find ourselves in the situations we inhabit today.

Prayer

So, before we dive in, let's pray. Praying when we do not know how to start, face uncertainty, or do not really see the way ahead can be hard. Here is one of my scribblings from a period which felt like this. (It might remind you of a prayer of Thomas Merton's, which I also often use personally but I believe I am not allowed to reproduce without due to copyright issues. His is more eloquent if you would like to find it.)

My dear dear Lord, where are you now?
There are so many times when I feel blind, or blinded,
or at the very least fogged;
When all seems shrouded, the light is low,
the world is hazy and unclear.
The path goes on, but even the next turn is beyond my sight.

I came to all this without seeing
that all that might be part of it,
as my searching heart glimpsed the dawning of hope;
that I knew; I know; I hold; I seek;
I think. I believed. I hoped.
This was my call, my duty... dare I name it 'joy'?
I failed to spot the meaning of 'faith'
in your invitation to faith,
I think
I was sold a myth of certainty.
Or at least this was what I snatched at

hungered for
grabbed
and hoarded.

But now I look,
and faith without faith is no faith at all.
I cannot fully know,
but I am fully known.

In trust there is freedom
when there is freedom to trust.

In you there is life, whether or not I can see it,
and herein lies
my trust
my faith
my freedom
my life.

And yet, not mine, not fully, not yet
your trust
your faith
your freedom
your life.

Sufficient unto today is the grace herein.

BOOK ONE: CLINGING TO THE CROSS

1 - REFLECTION

You might like to listen to this before reading on
(it was designed to be heard more than read),
but it's up to you.

I could almost hear the call to midday prayer in that awful momentary stillness.

From the temple? It could have been the bells of the parish church ringing for the eucharist, or the scurrying monastic feet slipping in before the Abbot began to notice repeated tardiness, or the labourer pausing with bait box in hand to glance upwards as he ate giving thanks for God's provision. Not that I knew about those things, it was just that it all felt like it could have been, on that day as time paused and the universe reset itself.

On that day when the midday sun shone like a searchlight, like a strip light, like a flash light, like a breaking light as he climbed, and succumbed, and never once complained.

The light that somehow shattered the orderliness that we soldiers love so much, which scoffed at each hammer blow as if mocking the futile impact of metal upon metal upon flesh upon wood.

The light which gazed unblinking and stood witness to the elevation of the one among the two who was so completely with and so utterly other.

The light which embraced him, and them, and all the thems that ever could be, and even me.

I am other, you see. A foreigner. An invader. A man of

violence. An imposer of orders and order. I am despised but I am necessary.

And in this place it all crumpled in on itself... no, on him... no, through him.

It should have crushed him.

We should have crushed him.

We did crush the others, but he just took it, and it all reshaped around him as he hung in agony and cried out asking God why he had forsaken...

That should have crushed him... but he was looking further than I could see... farther on in beyond even the blazing glare of that sunlight, which itself was snuffed from the sky: all-consuming yet utterly insufficient.

And the order was changed.

The man became a son, the woman a mother.

The thief became a penitent.

And I... I don't know how to say it.

I don't know if I want to say it, in case it shatters.

And yet I knew. I saw. I suddenly understood.

I became welcome.

Surely this man was the son of God.

2 - THE CROSS: THE WAY OF FAITH

It all comes back to the cross: it always has and it always will. That "lightning rod of grace[6]" which crosses the uncrossable chasm between us and God and reconciles the irreconcilable in eternal hope. As we celebrate Communion in different churches and contexts week by week, we often hear the phrase 'He opened wide his arms upon the cross' as part of the Eucharistic Prayer. Rarely do I rush those words as in them I glimpse anew the breadth of those arms. Whenever I come to the Lord's Table I stumble once again into the astonishing truth that all is and all are held in this place. However much I may have struggled with this person or that one, this situation or another one, with myself, or with imagined issues over the last few days, all of this and all of them are embraced in the One who hung on that cross outside Jerusalem two millennia ago.

The cross is the most remarkable place; it is not so much that everyone is included but more that everyone can be included. God will never force himself on us, but is patient beyond comprehension and gracious beyond reason: we can walk away but we will never be pushed away.

> *If God is for us, who can be against us?... Who will bring any charge against those whom God has chosen? It is God who justifies. Who then is the one who condemns? No one. Christ Jesus who died—more than that, who was raised to life—is at the right hand of God and is also interceding for us... No, in all these things we are more than conquerors through him who loved us. For I am convinced that neither death nor life, neither angels nor demons, neither the present nor the future, nor any powers, neither height nor depth, nor anything else in all*

---

[6] Quote ascribed to AW Tozer, although I can only find secondary sources.

creation, will be able to separate us from the love of God that is in Christ Jesus our Lord.[7]

The cross: my working definition

The more I talk about it, the more clearly I see that my working explanation of the cross (by which I mean the thing that I would say to someone who asked me why it mattered to me if we were chatting in a pub or a bikers' café) is something like this: on the cross we see God in Christ refusing to let go of two irreconcilable things. He will not let go of you and me, despite our brokenness, our selfishness, our greed, our stubbornness, and so on. At the same time he will not let go of the perfect One who is God, his Father, the creator and sustainer of all that is and ever will be. Even though perfection and imperfection cannot possibly be brought together, he will not let go. Even though love and hatred will not mix, he will not let go. Even though it will almost literally tear him apart, he will not let go... and in his sacrifice, in his own body, he reconciles the two. Hold on to Jesus and there is hope, peace, a future, and a home, for he will never let go. This is the cross in all its mystery, grace, majesty, and hope.

One of many things that this means, I think, for those who are called to take up our own cross, is that we, too, are called to stand in the gap between those people and positions that seem irreconcilable, and to do so with hope. This is gospel living, and this is why I say that I think our debates about sexuality are, in part, a way into a bigger thing that God is teaching us. We have many things about which we disagree. We already noted the conflict between what one might call the traditional faith position of the church and the faith-position of the western world in terms of gender politics, sexuality, and self-identity. (I think that we can only really understand these as faith positions: both of them go beyond logic, science, history, or

[7] From Romans 8.31-29 NRSVA

even personal preference and are held in a realm where decisions have been taken that choose to trust something which cannot be empirically proven.) I also realise that this is a spectrum rather than a binary debate, of course, but think that the basic point I am pondering holds true even in increasing complexity. We will note below disagreement about the place of women in the church, or the right stage to baptise. We could discuss abortion rights, our views on genetic modification, our politics, or any one of a number of matters. This is not a single issue question.

Inhabiting a divided world

This way of understanding the cross, though, does offer a way into the tensions amongst which we live.

We might disagree as to the cause of any one division, but it is clear that there are many things that we allow to divide us, even though they are actually good things in themselves. Some prioritise the Bible (or the traditions that have arisen from our interaction with it) above all things, whilst others prioritise acceptance and affirmation of others; expressing this in black and white seems uncontroversial but these two goods lead to division in practice (at least sometimes). Some will place sung worship at the centre of faith, whilst for others it will be service, or intercession, or preaching; again, all of these are good but they can end up separating people into tribes. I could go on; these things are good in themselves, and most of us will want to claim that we are loving, balanced, and sensible, and would never seek to be divisive. There is a problem here, though, as we might not be seeing ourselves with perfect clarity.

Let me risk being blunt in order to make my point: each of us tend to see ourselves as full of both grace and truth, but we are sometimes able to notice that others are rather less balanced and nuanced than us. Jesus described this as noticing the speck in your brother's eye whilst failing to spot the log in your own[8]. Division often looks like someone else's fault, and this could be a problem. However, noticing this temptation to 'blame' others can be turned to our advantage if we are prepared to be humble, robust, and honest. It means that noticing the shape of another's eye-speck may give you a handle on the log you carry around.

Choose any division and it can seem that the gap between 'camps' only gets bigger as the issue becomes clearer. If we take the issue of sexuality, given that this is our way in, it is hard to see common ground, in practice, between those who start with a traditional understanding of the Bible, and those who begin with the breadth of experience in the modern world. Is there a middle ground between the stones and the firelight? Can we hold to both truth and grace? Or is this merely the wishful thinking of a troubled Anglican bishop?

My family faith-roots are in the Plymouth Brethren to which all four of my grandparents belonged. The 'closed' brethren, of which my family were never really a part, separate themselves from others to the greatest possible degree. They will not eat with outsiders or spend any time that is not essential with anyone who does not belong. Where possible children are sent to Brethren schools, and even the meeting halls are built without windows at street level so that people can neither see out nor in. Over the years, I have repeatedly heard people quoting 2 Corinthians 6.17 (in which St Paul refers back to verses in the Hebrew Scriptures such as Isaiah 52.11 and Ezekiel 20.34,41), '*Come ye out and be ye separate*'.

The Brethren methodology is clear. We are to gather to ourselves, disengage from the world, and wait out the rest of this created order that the Lord may find us faithful when he returns. I remember, as a boy struggling to understand this, asking my father how the Brethren engage in the mission to which Christ commissions his followers. '*By breeding*' was his

---

[8] See Matthew 7.3-4

wry and thoughtful response. It didn't satisfy me then, and doesn't now, to think that faithfulness to Christ could be embodied by withdrawal from the world, which feels rather more like abandonment and isolation than loving participation in the missio-Dei. Obviously the Closed Brethren model is a bit of a paper tiger as few would agree with them today and their numbers appear to be small and declining. In practice, though, their approach might be extreme but it is far from unique in today's church and I am not sure we should be at ease with this.

If that approach is not right, though, does the pendulum need to swing to the other extreme? Do we simply flip the coin in terms of our missional engagement in the world? If the Christian vocation and responsibility is more than simply to be present, does this mean that the Christian may participate in every part of life? *'All things are permissible for me'*, says the apostle after all (1 Corinthians 6.12), even if he then goes on to observe that *'not everything is beneficial.'* I live under grace not law, and therefore I can be in any situation and walk alongside anyone. This much is surely true, but the pendulum of popular Christian culture would swing further in this direction, and suggest that we may inhabit whichever lifestyle we feel most fulfils our humanity. Rules, after all, are part of the old covenant not the new. Is this any more defensible that the separatist position?

Certainly, there is much to be said for an incarnational model of ministry which encourages and enables Christians to be present in every part of society in order that the hope of new life in Christ might be offered to all. Jackie Pullinger is an example to us all, for example, in the way she walked into Kowloon's walled city and embodied Good News. She did not, however, engage in the drug habits, violence, or prostitution of those to whom she had been sent. Clearly there are extremes on this side of the argument that would concern us too. I simply don't believe that it is possible to be a Christian human-trafficker or pimp, although it is the most beautiful and

...erful event when such people become Christians and ... that process of letting Jesus bring full conversion of life.

...pace between withdrawal and surrender

...the point, but suspect that I don't need to over-egg it as ...d be commonly held, at least in theory. We neither wish ...draw from the world in holy fear nor engage in every ...within the world in unholy abandon, but there is a large ...ground in between. The question is how we might ...this as faithful witnesses and disciples, embodying both ...and presence for the sake of the mission of God and in ...at we might live in a healthy, holy, and fulfilled manner. ...entic call of the Christian is to be *'in the world, but not* ...e present but distinct, to be *'aliens and strangers'* with ...ip in heaven but a right of abode on earth. This is ...y, morally, and relationally complex, and much of the writing in the New Testament addresses itself to the question of how we do this well. Living in one world in a manner which engages and thrives, whilst remaining a faithful citizen of another is always going to lead to internal tension. We see it in the story of the people of God throughout the Bible and over the span of history. The easy and simplistic response of exclusive faithfulness to one world or the other simply does not work. It seems to me that we are called to the painful daily tension of holding both worlds in our very existence as an act of worship, redemption, and intercession, before the throne of grace, and in so doing to incarnate in some small way the very presence of God in the darkest places in the world.

And this really (like really, really) matters! I want to argue in the strongest possible terms that this in-between space is deeply Christ-like and authentic. Pretty much every bit of my understanding of Christ, my Christology as we called it, points me in this direction.

Jesus' identity

Who is Jesus, after all? John tells us right at the start of his gospel that he is *'the Word'* and that he is with God, he is God, he is the One through whom all things were created, and that he *'became flesh and lived among us[9]'*. Jesus is God, and he is utterly human living right in the midst of humanity. In his very body he holds together divinity and humanity. It is no wonder that St Paul will later affirm that *'He himself is our peace, who has made us both one and has broken down in his flesh the dividing wall of hostility by abolishing the law of commandments expressed in ordinances, that he might create in himself one new man in place of the two, so making peace, and might reconcile us both to God in one body through the cross...[10]'*. In Jesus' very body, person, and nature we see the seeds of reconciliation as he inhabits the Kingdom of God within and alongside the rebellious empires of this world.

Jesus' ministry

We see this pattern throughout his ministry as Jesus allows himself to be associated with sinners, with tax collectors and prostitutes, hypocrites, murderers, liars, thieves, and pretty much everyone who will come to him. The religious hated it, and hate him, for it. As Jesus observes, *'the Son of Man has come eating and drinking, and you say, "Look, a glutton and a drunkard, a friend of tax collectors and sinners!"[11]'* Yet in this place he speaks of holiness and salvation which goes beyond anything they had imagined. He does not condemn the woman caught *'in the very act of adultery[12]'*, but neither does he leave her in her life of sin. In his works of deliverance and healing we glimpse the wonderful collision of the power and presence of

---

[9] See John 1 for both of these references.
[10] Ephesians 2.14-16a ESVUK
[11] Luke 7.34 NRSVA
[12] See John 8

God with the brokenness and captivity of this world, and the liberation that results.

And the pattern does not stop as Jesus ascends to his Father, where he is now, at the right hand of God interceding for the world[13], for you and me. Jesus is seated at the right hand of the Father, interceding in love. This is the icon of which our current discipleship is a kind of devoted mirror image as we are called to be at the right hand of creation calling out in worship to the God that humanity has corporately rejected but who still holds us in faithful hope. Stand back in your imagination and look afresh on this beautiful image of the parted lovers calling out across an apparently unbridgeable divide, knowing that their destiny is to be united... and wonder anew at the salvific power of the narrative: Christ himself has closed the gap. He and we are separate for now, but only because he has gone ahead to prepare a place for us to be at home. But, in the now, we are here in the place of missional engagement. We are in the world but not of it, but very much still in it because we are in Christ whose arms are still extended and who just will not let go.

Jesus' crucifixion

Perhaps above all in his crucifixion, we see Jesus refusing to deny his identity or turn his back on the created order. He refuses to release his grip either of the Father or of this world. There are so many important metaphors to help us begin to understand the cross and each of them matters[14]. This one, though, is beautifully simple and deeply visual (which matters in a world that is shaped by images) and captures truth profoundly. The cross is the place in which Christ holds on to the world with one hand, and God with the other and thus makes the two one in his own flesh. *'For he is our peace; in his flesh he has made both groups into one and has broken down the*

---

[13] We see this in the latter part of Romans 8, for example.
[14] John Stott's seminal work, *The Cross of Christ*, explores this so much more fully than I would ever be able to.

dividing wall, that is, the hostility between us.[15]*.* His body is stretched to breaking point and the eternal creator is pinned to an insubstantial bit of dead wood by his refusal to let go of one side or the other of the otherwise unbridgeable eternal chasm. He himself is (quite literally) our peace.

> *He himself is before all things, and in him all things hold together. He is the head of the body, the church; he is the beginning, the firstborn from the dead, so that he might come to have first place in everything. For in him all the fullness of God was pleased to dwell, and through him God was pleased to reconcile to himself all things, whether on earth or in heaven, by making peace through the blood of his cross.*[16]

Take up your own cross and follow

Moreover, this is not only the central salvific action in all history, it is also the distinctive, foundational, and central Christian vocation. This calling is clear in the New Testament, in the arc of the narrative of God's mission in the world, and in the missional instructions of Christ. We are not permitted to abandon the world he loves any more than he was prepared to abandon us. He loved and loves his creation and reaches out repeatedly, determinedly, and patiently in order that his children might come home. If God does not withhold his own Son, how are his children ever going to be called to withhold themselves from his missional purposes of love? I love the way one of the great eucharistic prayers of the Church of England describes God as drawing us into his covenant of grace 'again and again' even when we choose the path of rebellion: he will not abandon us, for we are his[17].

In the light of our conversation so far, it is no wonder that this is a really tough place to be. The Bible and those around us

---

[15] Ephesians 2.14 NRSVA
[16] Colossians 1.17-20 NRSVA
[17] See Eucharistic prayer F by following little-house-in-joppa.uk/S&F202333

appear to be pulling in different directions on many different levels. If we refuse to let go of the Father or the world we, too, will be stretched to a point which may not appear to be containable within our limited created order. We will face breakage, and thus a very simple choice: will we let go and head off in one direction or will we cling on to both knowing that in so doing we can never hold them together? Only a fool would choose the latter path, were it not for a deep conviction that this is the Christian vocation which enables the redemptive work that only God can complete. It is only in this cross-shaped approach, working through the very brokenness which marks his fallen creation, that we see God's salvation beginning to dawn. In this light the question of wisdom begins to look a little different, for *'God's foolishness is wiser than human wisdom, and God's weakness is stronger than human strength*[18].*'*

We are called to be just such a crucified people. Paul claims of himself that *"I have been crucified with Christ; and it is no longer I who live, but it is Christ who lives in me*[19].*"* Whilst this verse is set within the context of his own wrestling with the sin he finds within himself, it is a key concept for Christian theology. The redeemed sinner abides with the saviour in the place of salvation. It is both a discipline and our vocation to be in this place of redemption, reckoning, and painful hope if we are to walk the way of the cross-carrying Christ who told his disciples that *"'If any want to become my followers, let them deny themselves and take up their cross and follow me. For those who want to save their life will lose it, and those who lose their life for my sake will find it.*[20]*"*

Completing Christ's sufferings

Paul goes further, though. Like so many before me, I have long pondered his rather opaque assertion in Colossians 1 following the passage I quote above, when he says that *"in my flesh I am*

[18] 1 Corinthians 1.25 NRSVA
[19] Galatians 2.19-20, NRSVA
[20] Matthew 16.24-25, NRSVA

completing what is lacking in Christ's afflictions for the sake of his body, that is, the church."[21]. How, I wonder, can the apostle regard the messianic sacrifice as in some manner insufficient? It is a core doctrine of orthodox Christianity, that on the cross, Christ made *"(by his one oblation of himself once offered) a full, perfect, and sufficient sacrifice, oblation, and satisfaction for the sins of the whole world*[22]*"* and yet Paul seems clear that this work needs completing or filling. How are we to understand this?

Look at the flow of the apostle's thought in this chapter (italics mine and for clarity of argument):

- Paul expresses his gratitude for the Colossians' faith in Christ and love for the saints, and their hope which is *laid up in heaven* (4-5)
- The gospel *bears fruit and grows* in the whole world and has done so among the Colossian believers *since they truly comprehended the grace of God* (6)
- Paul's prayer for them to be filled with wisdom, live lives worthy of the Lord, and be made strong being prepared to endure everything with patience (9-12)
- Paul's focus is on Christ, who:
  - Has rescued us from the power of darkness (13-14)
  - Is fully and completely God (15-19)
  - Makes peace *in his blood* on the cross and reconciles *in his fleshly body* on the cross (20-22)
- It is in this context that Paul rejoices in his own sufferings and *in his flesh* completes Christ's sufferings (24a)
- This completion of Christ's suffering is *for the sake of his [Christ's] body*, the church (24b)
- In order that the mystery of the word of God may be known and all may hear (25-28)

The work of Christ, in his very body, was the reconciliation of heaven and earth, God and humanity. Paul has been called to

---

[21] Colossians 1.24, NRSVA
[22] Book of Common Prayer (1662) Eucharistic Prayer

serve, proclaim, and even continue this work, and it is in this light that he sees the hardships through which his own body goes as he gives himself to ministering the Good News that Jesus makes possible on the cross. It is clear that they are an echo of the crucifixion through which he has been saved, but he says more than this; he sees them as part of the salvific work of Christ which lies in the remit of the apostle not only of the saviour. Here is a remarkable glimpse into the methodology of our God who chooses never to work alone, and for the sake of our thinking here let's examine this and not brush it under the corner of a theological rug.

Any serious reader of the New Testament will be aware that Paul's faith rests in the cross and resurrection of Jesus Christ. This is the sufficient, eternal, perfect work of salvation worked by the Trinitarian Godhead in order that humanity might be rescued from sin and darkness. There can be no sense, if the apostle is consistent as we believe him to be, that he is undermining this core doctrine. However, there is something important in this verse that we ignore at our peril, for it shines light on the manner in which the Father works, and it draws us into Christlike and authentic discipleship; discipleship which takes seriously our Lord's command to be carriers not only of *the* cross but of *our* cross.

Paul's argument seems to be that, in some manner at least, he participates in the saving work of God by placing himself in a position where his own life bridges the divide between the *"power of darkness"* from which we are rescued in Christ and the *"grace of God"* into which we are invited in Christ. In pictorial form, it is as if his calling in Christ is to cling with one hand to God and with the other to the people and communities to which he is sent and of which he is part. He belongs to Christ, but Christ's love for the world is stronger than we can comprehend and Paul is bound in service of this love. He is not to loose his grip on either as he stands in this place of both intercession and embodied proclamation until such a time as Christ returns to bring the work he has begun to completion. It is Paul's very refusal to let go of either that enables his vocation and ministry, and which leads him to a place of suffering in his own flesh. And, of course, this vocation reflects the cruciform calling of Christ himself. This embodied proclamation of the work of the saviour is entrusted to those who follow in the cross-laden footsteps of the Christ, and such announcement of the love of God is no mere work of broadcasted theory. Gospel proclamation is offered in the vernacular and in person; it will risk body and even soul to proclaim gospel grace, as the disciple chooses the path of obedient identification and service and follows Christ in making the journey of love which the lost are unable to make for themselves. The apostle is never truly apostolic until it is only the hand of Christ that holds them from the death-embrace of the grasping hands of darkness, as they refuse to let go of either in the hopeful faith that their hands held out are the very hands of the Christ to whom they cling.

Moreover, this work in Paul's flesh is, as he says, for the sake of the body of Christ. By this he means the church, as he tells us, but why does he not simply say *"in my flesh I am completing what is lacking in Christ's afflictions for the sake of the church."*? There seem to be deliberate connotations being implanted here. Christ suffered in his body on the cross as he bridged the chasm between humanity and the grace of God. He sends apostles to embody and proclaim this good-news-message in their own flesh, for the sake of his body, the church, who are shaped and called to do that very same work of being a bridge-head into the fallen order. This is the place and calling of the church, and of the disciple in every age. We, too, cling to Christ with one hand and the world with the other even though this stretches us on the cross we carry. It is our calling in and for this age, and whilst we hold eternally assured hope that our citizenship is beyond this place and our destiny is secured we may not climb down from the place and message of salvation until the day of resurrection. We are *in but not of* this world, not merely because this is some kind of waiting room as the master physician completes his treatment of creation, but rather because our very being is part of that treatment.

The shared nature of cross-carrying

Moreover, this shared nature of the body of Christ opens our eyes to the individualism with which we usually read Scriptures that were written in a communal culture. Paul had a particular calling as a particular apostle. Whilst it is true that there are elements of cross-carrying that we will do alone, never forget that we, together, are the body of Christ and together we carry the cross and bear each other's burdens. This is a shared calling not merely an isolated or individual one.

This is a dangerous and costly calling; it is far easier to let go of one side or the other, but to do so would be to step outside the grace of God and risk losing the very salvation we proclaim. It is a calling which might, in itself, seem to place our very soul at risk as we are pulled hither and thither by the world we are called to love and serve, but this place of embodiment is the way of the cross, and thus the path of sharing in salvation. The way of discipleship is clear as we cling to Christ in worship, obedience, prayer, and study of his word; we live, we love, we pray, and in our very flesh we carry the discomfort and inconsonance. It is the burden of the faithful to bear if we will partake in the calling and work of Christ; the lost do not carry it for us or sort themselves out so that we may lay it down. (We shall return to this thought below.)

The comfort and strength of cross-carrying

Before we move on let me share one other thought that brings me strength on my hardest days. Peter wrestles with this call to live well in a divided world, even to the extent of accepting ungodly authority. His rationale for doing so is Christ's own suffering and the manner in which he conducts himself. It is in this context that he says, '[Jesus] himself bore our sins in his body on the cross, so that, free from sins, we might live for righteousness; by his wounds you have been healed[23].'

---

[23] 1 Peter 2.24 NRSVA

I love one of the implications of this, although I fully recognise that this is not the primary meaning of this text: when I find myself stretched to breaking in the service of Christ, recognising that at least part of the reason that this is so hard is because of my own brokenness, nevertheless I see that in giving myself to the crucified life I am simply casting myself into the arms of the One who is eternally crucified. In my small suffering, I find myself embraced in his once-for-all suffering, and somehow this makes it all possible. His wounds take the sting for my wounds, his brokenness holds my brokenness, and in this place of discipleship I find not only obedience, mission, and devotion, but also strength, healing, and grace.

These themes of cross-carrying, of embodying the crucifixion, of being a people created and defined by the cross, are themes Paul returns to. When he is arguing with the Galatian Christians about whether they are saved by doing what the law says, by following a strict holiness code, he points to the saviour as crucified: *'You foolish Galatians! Who has bewitched you? It was before your eyes that Jesus Christ was publicly exhibited as crucified!*[24]*'*, but also asserts:

> *I have been crucified with Christ; and it is no longer I who live, but it is Christ who lives in me. And the life I now live in the flesh I live by faith in the Son of God, who loved me and gave himself for me*[25].

It is the way of the cross which is the way of salvation. We cannot let go of one side or the other of the salvation equation, however much it might be easier if we did. Paul wrestles with this as he ponders how wonderful it would be to die and be with Christ, but how necessary it is for the sake of the mission of God (seen in this context in and through the Philippian church) that

---

[24] Galatians 3.1 NRSVA
[25] From Colossians 1.19-20 NRSVA

he remains in the flesh for now. 'For me, to live is Christ and to die is gain[26]', as he expresses it.

We should not expect this to be easy, and this is why it demands huge discipline. Listen again to Paul's teaching addressed to the Church in Colossae:

> So, if you have been raised with Christ, seek the things that are above, where Christ is, seated at the right hand of God. Set your minds on things that are above, not on things that are on earth, for you have died, and your life is hidden with Christ in God. When Christ who is your life is revealed, then you also will be revealed with him in glory.
>
> Put to death, therefore, whatever in you is earthly: fornication, impurity, passion, evil desire, and greed (which is idolatry). On account of these the wrath of God is coming on those who are disobedient. These are the ways you also once followed, when you were living that life. But now you must get rid of all such things—anger, wrath, malice, slander, and abusive language from your mouth. Do not lie to one another, seeing that you have stripped off the old self with its practices and have clothed yourselves with the new self, which is being renewed in knowledge according to the image of its creator. In that renewal there is no longer Greek and Jew, circumcised and uncircumcised, barbarian, Scythian, slave and free; but Christ is all and in all!
>
> As God's chosen ones, holy and beloved, clothe yourselves with compassion, kindness, humility, meekness, and patience. Bear with one another and, if anyone has a complaint against another, forgive each other; just as the Lord has forgiven you, so you also must forgive. Above all, clothe yourselves with love, which binds everything together in perfect harmony. And let the peace of Christ rule in your hearts, to which indeed you were called in the one body. And be thankful. Let the word of Christ dwell in you richly; teach and admonish one another in all wisdom; and with gratitude in your hearts sing psalms, hymns, and spiritual songs to God. And whatever you do, in

---

[26] Philippians 1.21 NRSVA

word or deed, do everything in the name of the Lord Jesus, giving thanks to God the Father through him.[27]

The costly discipline of cross-carrying

We will return to this, but I confess that I find myself increasingly troubled in this regard around human sexuality. I see clearly where the popular mind and heart seems to be heading in these questions, and intuitively grasp the sense that this is about love. It concerns me that, when we talk about love, we often seem to have nothing distinctive to say and seem only to be preaching acceptance despite understanding ourselves to be the people of the God who is love. At the same time I see the effect that much of our proclamation of scriptural clarity with regard to sexuality has beyond the walls of the church (whichever 'side of the debate' is being heard). We will think, at the start of book 2, about the task of communication, but it worries me that we believe we are proclaiming love and yet we are heard to be proclaiming either nothing or, at times, hate. And, more than this, every conversation about this seems to lead to anger, division, and rancour, rather than to peace, holiness, joy, and Christ.

Might it be that we are missing our costly and complicated vocation in all of this, through a good desire to embrace that which we know of God. What might it mean, I ask, to hold to both Christ and the world?

Whatever it might mean, it will be costly, difficult, and painful. One of the little exercises I find myself drawn to in this is to use the seven words Jesus spoke from the cross as a kind of shaping of prayer and reflection. St Ignatius of Loyola describes a discipline called *Lectio Divina* (a 'divine reading' of Scripture) in which we sit in the presence of the text and allow ourselves to be immersed in it. As we draw to the end of this chapter, why

---

[27] Colossians 3.1-17 NRSVA

not try it with these words as we seek to be faithful to the calling of a cross-carrier.

Father, forgive them, for they know not what they do. (Luke 23.34) Perhaps this provides a manner to pray for those with whom we struggle and who threaten our own spiritual well-being. It offers a way to hold others before the throne of grace without the need to approve of them or their actions... but beware, as I often find that when I start in just such a place I end by confessing that I, too, need deep forgiveness. I might be called to participate in the work of Christ, but I am still very far from sharing in his perfection.

Truly, I say to you, today you will be with me in paradise. (Luke 23.43) For me, this 'word' shapes my prayers in line with the ultimate purpose into which we are called, namely that of mission. What we are, and how we behave matters and it matters eternally. This person, this situation, looks different in the light of eternity and if I can spot this, I pray and live differently.

Woman, behold your son. Son, behold your mother. (John 19.26-27) Here we are called into new community; into new relationship that sustains, holds and nurtures. This is part of the gift of God in the foretaste of his new creation. We cannot bear our cross alone, and are not normally called to do so. Pray for, and with community that carries a shared cross.

My God, My God, why have you forsaken me? (Matthew 27.46 & Mark 15.34) This is costly and there will be times we feel abandoned and alone. This is part of the Biblical pattern of prayer and worship, and we glimpse it here just as we see it throughout the Psalms. Lament matters when you carry a cross, and we need to find ways to express and explore this. We will return to this later in our journey together (at the end of book 2) as it matters, and probably matters more than we will glimpse.

I thirst. (John 19.28) We have a real need for sustenance, physical, emotional, mental, and spiritual. Such need is not somehow unholy, and we are not normally meant to bear it alone. We need to learn to ask for the Lord to meet this need, and then to trust him to provide well and in good time.

It is finished/done/complete. (John 19.30) I love this: Christ has done it. We can trust, be at peace and confident whatever we face... he holds it and he holds us.

Father, into thy hands I commit my spirit. (Luke 23.46) ... and so, in the meantime, we trust in him absolutely, completely, and with all we are and do.

2A — PAUSING FOR BREATH

_____

Pause for a moment and consider...

What issues are you wrestling with that have caused you to pick up this book?

If the following questions are useful, please use them to reflect:

1) What have I noticed the Spirit of saying to me in this chapter?
   a) What have I learned?
   b) Where do I want to reflect further?
   c) What ideas will not go away?
2) What does the cross actually mean for me (in practice) today?
3) How can I share in cross carrying alongside my sisters and brothers in Christ?
4) What do I need to do in response to what God is saying to me?

3 – DEVALUING THE CROSS

As we have said, it all comes back to the cross; that old rugged cross, the emblem of suffering and shame[28]...

... but here we go. We will come back to the amazing blessings of the cross in the next chapter, but first we ought perhaps, to pause and consider the shadows that we can so easily inhabit, even around our thinking about the cross. We need to explore, we need to understand, but we do not need to live in condemnation... in fact the bible is clear that we should not live in condemnation.

As soon as I type words from the hymn above, I am conflicted. I hear the tune in my head and my heart both lifts and sinks in the same moment. Bennard and Mullins' hymn is an enduring favourite, even appearing in Dr Who in 2009 (which must be among the highest of accolades). The tune is hauntingly beautiful, and the words have the echo of profundity and longing. I have lost count of the number of funerals I have taken in which this hymn has been requested. But herein is an illustration of part of the problem with the way we interact with the cross. It has become so commonplace in our world that we do not think about it (and we would be wise to note that we are as much at danger of this as anyone else). It is rare to pass a jeweller's shop without seeing cross necklaces, cross earrings, and cross pendants for sale, yet it is unlikely (at best) that all those who walk around wearing that jewellery have a real comprehension of what it means.

---

[28] Words from 'The Old Rugged Cross', George Bennard and Catherine Mullins' famous hymn of 1912.

Before we consider this in greater detail, though, let me observe two things.

Firstly, any time spent considering the cross of Jesus Christ is well spent and almost always beneficial. You cannot engage, even in the most fundamentally flawed manner, with this most powerful and intimate engagement of God the creator with his broken creation without being affected. Do not despise the fruit of such reflection, even if it is not complete, full, or entirely accurate. *And here, let me add a further health warning especially for the most diligent of readers: it would be very easy to beat yourself up in this or the parallel chapters in books two and three of this series. Please try not to as that really is not what they are here for. Trust me when I assert that any time spent at the foot of the cross is good time, and then search for the freedom to spot ways we might focus our attention more tightly or clearly. We look at the problems so we can work through them not so we can be further bound by them.*

Secondly, please be wary when you take the cross for granted, when you reduce it to functionalism, when you make it more about you than about Jesus, when you ignore it, or when you are tempted to skirt around it. Don't pretend that you are not tempted to do so (the fact that you want to do so tells you something really important) but do push through and come back to this place of grace. I am not suggesting you will do these things specifically, but if your reflection on the cross does not lead you to some of these places then I respectfully suggest you might not be reflecting deeply enough.

Having described the basic idea behind this chapter (that each of us needs to take care as we will all domesticate the cross in our own ways), I offer various further things to you. These are offered by way of starting a conversation not ending one, offered despite being both subjective and reflective. What I want to encourage (to be honest, I want to encourage in myself as much as in anyone else), is a habit of reflexivity that notices when we wander off track and stop living at the foot of the cross.

Please don't get worked up or overly bothered though: as I say above, spending time before the cross is always beneficial, good, and usually holy. However, just because you are looking at the cross does not mean that you are seeing all that you can or should yet see: you rarely remain static in this place because God is always drawing you in and on and up and deeper (I know that sounds illogical, but this is how the bigness of God feels sometimes[29]). Keep wondering, learning, growing, and glimpsing both from your 'mistakes' and your insights.

There are many limited ways that we can respond to the cross, and we would be wise to note this with humility. Here I shall mention a few, but my 'list' will never be exhaustive.

Rose-tinting the cross

Have you noticed how easy it is to romanticise the cross?

It gets made into beautiful jewellery, stuck on the wall, pictured in front of sunsets, set to beautiful music, and embraced as if it were a psychological cuddly toy. It is all too easy to glance fondly in its direction and with no malice aforethought make it slushy, nice, beautiful, and purely symbolic. I recall one Sunday school lesson where the teacher turned an image of the cross through 45 degrees and told us it was God's kiss for the world... and at one level this is deeply true. The cross is, arguably, the ultimate expression of love. However, it is very far either from a romantic embrace or a kindly peck on the cheek.

If you walk around the North of England (and why wouldn't you?) you will see stunningly beautiful celtic crosses placed in gorgeous places. Holiday-makers and locals alike pause and take photos, and every so often someone may associate it with Christ or with Christianity. Few, though, pause to ponder why

---

[29] See Ephesians 3.18-19; this is not only me!

it (or a predecessor) would have been put there. The celtic Christians stuck the cross in places of beauty, I am told, as a sign and symbol that Christ's redemption was present and that the world needed it desperately. It was not a celebration of earthly beauty, but a symbol of God's inbreaking Kingdom, and that symbol is an instrument of execution, torture, and agony.

The cross is beyond beautiful but also unimaginably awful. It is part of every day of our history but, in being so, radically reshapes and redeems every day rather than simply ornamenting it. At a profound level the cross is peace, hope, freedom, and life... but only once we have ridden the storm of its defeat of the brokenness of the world. At the same time, the cross is wild, violent, radical, uncomfortable, and untameable; just as Aslan can never be understood as a tame lion[30], so the cross of Christ is the ultimate hard reality. When we come to the cross we are the ones who are reshaped, remade, and refound... and this matters when we come to living with disagreement. We should not expect that it will be easy, or that we have it 'right' when it is comfortable.

Learn to be wary when your grip on the cross becomes too familiar or easy. In particular, be alert lest you find yourself either assuming the cross does away with difficulty or hard bakes struggle into discipleship; it is much more real than either easy assumption would assert.

Be careful when you assume that the cross does away with conflict or struggle

One of the most common errors we fall into is assuming that God's Kingdom is with us in full already. Reading what we have already explored might give the impression that crucifixion means that Christians can now stand together without difficulty, challenge, or cost. This automatic or easy

---

[30] This is an image taken from CS Lewis' Narnia books, in which the lion, Aslan, is a metaphor for Christ. It is said of him that he is good, but should never be mistaken for a tame lion.

collaboration between those who follow Christ has never been the case[31] and I suspect that the cross shows that, at the very least, it will never be simple, completed, or able to be taken for granted. Reconciliation, unity, and grace are all costly.

Be careful when you assume that the cross means ongoing conflict

Equally, the fact that we are called to be cross-carriers does not mean that we should always assume we will be persecuted or in disagreement. People sometimes claim (in our pampered Western context) to be facing opposition for the sake of their faith only for others to suspect that they are facing opposition because they are being plain awkward or intransigent. Assuming confrontation often opens us up to making it more likely.

Taking the cross for granted

Have you noticed how easy it is to assume we somehow deserve the cross?

I wrestle with putting it this way because it feels so presumptuous to say, but is this not exactly what we do? We have known about what God did on the cross for as long as we can remember, and this simply becomes our understanding of his role. It's like the people who unblock sewers: an unpleasant job, to be sure, but someone has to do it. The cross needed to happen, Jesus drew the short straw, let's say a polite thank you and move on.

I probably have not captured the way you do this, but let me invite you to reflect: do you take the cross for granted? Do you assume that it will be there? Christians in Rome seem to have come to believe that they could sin as much as they liked because grace was always there for them[32]. Paul is adamant

---

[31] Acts 15.36-41 relates one example of this where even Paul and Barnabas fall out.

[32] I am referring here to Romans 6.1-2

that this logic cannot work: indeed, that we need to understand ourselves as crucified with Christ[33], not merely recipients of his doing the difficult work for us. It is impossible to inhabit grace when we take it for granted, and this matters enormously because we can only live well in complexity when we live the reality of grace daily.

Be wary when you no longer feel you need the cross.

Mastering the cross

Have you noticed how quickly we think we have understood or contained the cross?

We do this all the time with things that are familiar to us. We possess them rather than letting them possess us: even our language communicates this: *my* country, *my* friend, *my* service, *my* saviour... as if we were the lead agent in any of those partnerships. I fully recognise that describing something as 'mine' does not necessarily mean I possess it, except that it does often come dangerously close to doing so.

We all need to engage with the world in a manageable way. We often do this by recreating the world in our imagination and practising how we will do something. If I have messed up a practical task or lost an argument, I sometimes replay what I did in my head adjusting things 'til I work out what I think I should have done. If I am working out where to walk in town, I imagine the route. If I know I need to have a tough conversation with you, I practise it in my head with an imaginary you. If I am going to teach you to ride a motorbike, I work through how I shall approach each lesson (although I also improvise when we get to the actual event depending on how things play out in the real world). This is all good, unless our imaginary world becomes more real than the real world and we get stuck in it or in the behaviour it requires. I could be your very closest friend in my head, but if I never communicate with you it is not worth

---

[33] See Romans 6.6 (and the rest of chapter 6)

all that much (and might actually make me the antithesis of a friend in practice).

Be careful that you don't create such a model of the cross that you control it, limit it, constrain it, or tame it. Don't place barriers around it that exclude yourself or others. You are not custodian, you are disciple and worshipper, and the journey of devotion and liberation is constantly fresh and constantly beyond you (in the best sense).

Be careful when you only want to stand with those who share 'your' view of the cross

I urge particular caution here. Of course we won't agree with everyone who says they live life in the light of the cross, but we are in very dangerous territory indeed when a particular view or insight is the only permissible one for those with whom we are in fellowship. Unity in disagreement is really hard, particularly knowing when or where to draw lines of division. I am not arguing for a particular boundary here, but I am noting that protestants do divide easily and can seem to do so based on a judgement of other's views which the other party would not recognise. Two people who both look to the cross making that cross the point of their disunity is a very concerning matter, I think.

Be careful when others will only accept you if you agree with them

Equally, just as we need to avoid alienating others who do not completely agree with us, let me caution you lest you let others treat you in that way.

The cross is not specialist knowledge for the disciple of Christ, although there are always those who seek to make the message of the cross somehow hidden. When Paul warns the Galatian church not to turn aside to a different gospel[34], it is this

---

[34] Galatians 1.6-7

that he seems to have in mind as he confronts what is called 'gnosticism'. People have long claimed that there is hidden knowledge ('gnosis') that you need in order to understand the work of Christ and, thus (at least in part), the cross. It is not so; the cross is enough and all sufficient... indeed, as we are taken beyond ourselves it is often all that is sufficient.

Be wary when you stop being surprised by the cross or when it ceases to make demands of grace upon your life.

Ignoring an overly mysterious cross

Have you noticed how easy it is, bizarrely (given that we often do it at the same time as the last danger), to assume the cross is all mystery? We assume that we understand enough but that no one will ever understand all of it.

If the trouble with the last danger is that we recreate the cross according to our understanding, here the danger is that we simply ignore it whilst being grateful for its effect. It is like the engine in a modern car or the inner workings of a smartphone. We are delighted that they are there and glad to make use of them, but we are completely oblivious about how they actually work.

The trouble with this is that we cannot shape a life following Christ without taking seriously the call to take up our cross and follow him[35]; we must both be willing to be sent like lambs into the midst of wolves and to discover that the worker is worth their wages[36]. Write the cross off as mystery and we will, I suspect inevitably, either give ourselves an easy route to a cross-less unsacrificed spirituality, or style ourselves as the sacrificial lamb that only Christ can ever be. We either end up in prosperity and comfort gospel or seeking the route of martyrdom, either selfish or burned out, either self-pampering

---

[35] See Luke 9.23
[36] See Luke 10.3-7

or self-flagellating. Neither is desirable, and neither will solve the challenges we face.

It is, of course, true that we will never fully understand the mystery of the cross, but we understand a little more with each day we spend in its shadow, worshipping, wondering, and wrestling. We are formed a little deeper, shaped a little more completely, and released more fully to inhabit the image of Christ, our crucified Lord.

Be wary when you are tempted to take the easy way out in your wrestling with the cross.

'Using' the cross to support our inherent biases or preferences

There are so many ways we do this with the whole of the Bible, both theologically and socially, and it is really dangerous. There are all manner of things that we will think and feel in life; some will be right, others wrong, and most will be partly right. We need to be really careful when we ascribe biblical or theological rationales to things that are merely our, or our tribe's opinion or preference. We don't need to look far back to see Christianity being used to justify apartheid, or the suffering of Christ used to 'support' abusive behaviour.

This is a wider point, though, about the way we handle the Bible; each of us will be tempted, I suspect to ransack the Scriptures for evidence in support of our opinions. Even writing this chapter, I have chuckled at myself in this regard when making the point about the cross being misinterpreted by others. Instinctively I turned to 2 John, *'Everyone who does not abide in the teaching of Christ, but goes beyond it, does not have God; whoever abides in the teaching has both the Father and the Son.*[37]*'* This is teaching about being wary of those who proclaim a false gospel, but in context the concern is clearly about those

---

[37] 2 John 9 NRSVA

who deny the incarnation of Christ[38]. It would be so easy to gloss over this discrepancy between good exegesis and the point I am actually trying to make, but to do so not only presents something which might be erroneous (at least in part), it also potentially blinds us to a fuller and richer truth we are yet fully to explore.

Herewith my point: reflection on the cross will have implications for every area of our lives, but is rarely prescriptive of a particular position or view on matters which are tangential to its main, salvific, purposes. Let me give you some examples of ways we might make this mistake today based entirely on my own subjective observations (with which you may well disagree, of course, and you could be more right than me so please do feel guilt-free liberty if you do).

In search of freedom

Today, we tend to feel deeply the need to be free of oppressive external constraint. Unprocessed this can lead to a simplistic belief that any external constraint is damaging, and that freedom can in in someway be unlimited. There is widespread suspicion of institutions, expertise, and external absolute moral frameworks and this is not without good reason given some of the abuse scandals and societal inequity. This affects the way we vote, for example, or the way we feel our way through moral questions, and the way we discern our own identity.

The cross, and indeed the gospel, is clearly about freedom. *'For freedom Christ has set us free[39]'*, as Paul writes, but this freedom is not about licentiousness. Paul is equally clear:

> *I find it necessary to write and appeal to you to contend for the faith that was once for all entrusted to the saints. For certain intruders have stolen in among you, people who long ago were*

---

[38] 2 John 7-11 make it quite clear what the wider concern is, I think, as well as the response that we need.

[39] Galatians 5.1a NRSVA

> *designated for this condemnation as ungodly, who pervert the grace of our God into licentiousness and deny our only Master and Lord, Jesus Christ[40].*

Looking at the cross, we will not see independent freedom which allows us merely to self-define, but rather interdependent freedom which draws us into grace.

In search of authentic experience

Authenticity is deeply valued in the Western world, although it is also easily manipulated as the border between actual authenticity and felt authenticity does not appear to be clearly demarcated or well policed in the popular psyche (either in ourselves or in our perception of others). Indeed, the entertainment industry, arguably, have been working for years to break down this distinction and we will not always notice when we are being 'played'. This phenomena and this search are not new things, they are not necessarily *bad* things, but they *are* things and as such they bring strengths and weaknesses that we ought at least to note.

The search for authenticity might, for example, make some popular decision-making appear immature to those schooled in more reflective ways of thinking, but it is not necessarily simplistic, although neither is it finally determined by rational logic (any more than most decisions are, I suspect). The 'lines' of popular judgement seem clear to those of us who regularly imbibe at the fountain of popular media, but might be hard to determine for an outsider. The way we make decisions about abortion, or divorce when there are children involved, or any number of multi-layered moral situations illustrate the vast complexity with which we live all the time in this regard.

What, we might ask, could be more authentic than God's act of loving grace on the cross? The question is clearly right, but the danger is that we just stop having noticed it as if the experience of authenticity is all that matters. It isn't: there is much more to

---

[40] Jude 3b-4

explore and inhabit here. I guess the fact that you have got to this point in this text means you are alert to the danger of this, but we need to watch both our reception (and our communication) of the cross lest it becomes purely experiential and serves only to validate what appears good or right. Societal pressure may well push us in this direction and validate us when we respond, but the ongoing need for transformation by the renewal of mind is central to the calling of a disciple[41] and will always sit alongside our lived (and living) experience.

In search of acceptance

I sometimes think that the only near-universally agreed moral wrongs today are harming others or restraining another's freedom. The basic quality we value in those around us is that of accepting others as they are. None of us is (and nor could we possibly be) consistent in this, of course, as we rightly decry the racist, the sexist, the bigot, the snob, the discriminatory, the separatist, the elitist, or the ageist even as the politics of some types of separatism is on the rise. We accept everyone but live in a world which elects separatist, 'me-first' leaders even in the accepting and liberal West, and in which we are seeing a worrying rise of the 'far right' across Europe.

It is, nonetheless, a gut-level and basic assertion that we accept all, whatever their situation. At our best, we work for access for all. We want to make provision to allow for disability, maternity, gender, or religion. This is more than sympathy for those who have received a body, mind, culture, or social situation which might be seen to place them at a disadvantage when compared to an apparent norm in society. It is a choice to open access to all, so long as their difference doesn't cross a line which we feel rather than define, for there are some whose difference does not seem to be acceptable.

---

[41] See Romans 12.1, for a succinct example of this, but the point is made more generally and far more widely by the whole of the New Testament.

(Please note that this is a broad point making observation about the wider world in which we live. It is not a plea for any particular change. Let me give you a silly example: I think of a course I ran some years ago which involved me providing the meals. One person said they needed food without wheat or dairy, and were vegetarian. It was a tricky challenge (and expense) to find nourishing food for them, but I co-operated willingly and sympathetically. This changed in an instant when I saw them eating a brie sandwich made with the French bread I had provided for other course participants. They explained, when challenged, that this was good quality cheese in nice bread and the reason for their diet choice was simply a preference for better quality food. I was angry, but was I right to be? I judged them selfish and unkind, but in so doing revealed my judgement that the physical discomfort I thought I was avoiding as I prepared their food was more important to me than their mental discomfort. I still feel they crossed a line, but would never think that about a vegetarian who can eat meat but chooses not to... and in this I am not sure quite how robust the logic that I hold on to here is. There is a difference between serving a vegetarian and providing an access-ramp for a wheel-chair user, and yet I gladly adjust for both without clear guidance as to the distinction. I think I am just agreeing with those around me: we allow guide-dogs to enter shops, but require others to tie their canine friend up outside even if that animal is the one living being who provides significant assurance to someone with mental or emotional distress. Why do we make this judgement? If the pooch in question were some amazingly valuable hound we would simply tell the owner not to take it to the shop if they didn't want to risk it being stolen whilst it was left outside. This is a little ironic, now I think of it, given our normal obsession with money and happiness! The point I am making is that this is complex, it is often felt rather than thought, and it matters.)

Does the cross, which clearly extends an invitation to all whatever their situation or status, simply stand for acceptance? John 3.16 famously teaches us that *all* who believe in him may not perish but have eternal life: clearly we may not teach this and at the same time seek to exclude people from grace. However, neither may we teach only half of the truth, for John 3.16 comes with its own caveat, grace comes to those who believe (and the word does not only mean mental assent, it implies a choice to trust, follow, and obey). Acceptance is clearly central to the cost, but no proclamation of the gospel that omits the call to repentance stands the test of scrutiny.

In search of self-determination

Let me give a few quicker examples of various aspects of this search, starting with self-determination.

One of the consequences of all this is our permission to self-identify within limits (for example, I can choose my gender but not my race). Does the cross bring freedom from wrong constraints? Yes. Does it raise my own self-determination to some kind of absolutist reality? Not by any means, rather it invites us to discover more fully the way we have been created, and God is always the lead partner in this. Indeed Paul can write '*it is no longer I who live, but it is Christ who lives in me*[42]'.

In search of sexuality

I hesitate here, but we are obsessed with sex and sexuality today. It is no surprise to see that the cross is used to support our views here as well, and we do need to be aware of the question of which comes first: our views or the cross. I have not dared (and do not recommend) doing an internet search, but a quick look at JSTOR (which is a digital database of academic articles) reveals over 15,000 results in terms of articles exploring aspects of Christ's cross and our sexuality.

The fact that there are so many articles is a great illustration of the main point I am trying to make here. The cross will 'speak' into our sexuality in many ways, not least in terms of offering it

---

[42] Galatians 2.20 NRSVA written in the context of wrestling with wrestling with his sinful nature.

as part of our whole-person worship. 'Using' it, though, to support a particular view of sexual inclination or activity seems, at least to me, to step into biblically uncharted territory.

In search of tolerance

One of the wry observations about our culture today is that we tolerate everything except intolerance. Tolerance, arguably, is the highest virtue to which we can aspire... despite the fact that being tolerated is not exactly something to which any of us would aspire. Imagine coming to my house and me 'welcoming' you with an assurance that your presence will be tolerated! Herein a key distinction laid bare by the cross: the world might call for tolerance, the gospel offers grace.

There are so many other examples that we could give where we need to be careful how we are 'using' the cross: social justice, materialism, ecclesial traditions, to name but a few. Let me remind you, though, that my point is not that the cross is silent on these issues but rather than it is not a 'trump card' for a particular view. We need to be very careful about if we are tempted to employ it in our service rather than finding ourselves drawn into its orbit.

Make the cross out to be the only thing that Jesus did or cared about

Finally, in this snapshot, have you noticed how easy it is to make the cross into the only thing we ever talk about Jesus doing?

It will always be central, vital, and the lens through which we understand our faith, but we do sometimes give the impression that our Lord popped over for a long weekend to do the essentials: institute communion, weep a bit in Gethsemane, suffer a rotten trial, get crucified, and then leave us on the Sunday having let the women know that he was OK really.

I exaggerate, but we must see that the cross is set both in its biblical context and in the context of the incarnation, the whole life of Christ on both sides of his death and resurrection. The cross is key, but it is key partly because of the way that it engages with the whole of life and faith. I don't imagine I need to press this point, but we need to be just as wary if the cross is all we ever see of Jesus as we would need to be if we never spotted it in the first place. We, oddly, disempower the cross just as much by making it everything as making it nothing for in so doing we divorce it from the wider life and teaching of Christ.

I was once, some years ago, bold enough to express concern to the vicar of a large and popular church that the preaching at the Christmas services almost completely overlooked Jesus' birth in favour proclaiming his death. I tried to say that I was glad the cross was preached, but wondered what the gospel looked like when approached through the lens of the incarnation. I left the conversation feeling slightly sorry that I had mentioned it, but more convinced than ever that we need to be cautious if the only avenue we have in our understanding of grace is the cross. It will always be paradigmatic, central, and foundational. It is not (assuming we want to be biblical) divorced from other vital parts of the life of Christ, such as the incarnation, baptism, teaching, or Pentecost.

There are, of course, so many ways in which we need to take care (both sense in the sense of being wary and in the sense of allowing it to affect our hearts) in responding to the cross of Christ, and these are only some of them. Don't let me finish, though, without reminding you where we started this chapter: please do not live in fear of these things as if they are dreadful mistakes to make. Any reflection on the cross is better than none. Nobody will ever understand it fully, how could they? Consequentially all human reflections are flawed and partial, and we are wise to hold them lightly. Please do not allow this chapter (or the two parallel ones in the subsequent books) to become a burden, a stick to beat yourself (or others) with, a focal point that just irritates you, or something by which you feel you are being (or are going to be) judged. Come, rather, to worship, to grow, to wonder, and to find life: come and learn what God would teach you today, even though tomorrow you will learn more!

Let me repeat (because this is really vital and more true than we will ever fully grasp) that any and all time spent at the foot of the cross is time well spent.

3A – PAUSING FOR BREATH

Pause for a moment and consider...

What issues are you wrestling with that have caused you to pick up this book?

If the following questions are useful, please use them to reflect:

1) What have I noticed the Spirit of saying to me in this chapter?
   a) What have I learned?
   b) Where do I want to reflect further?
   c) What ideas will not go away?
2) Where (and how) am I in danger of diminishing the cross in my life?
3) Where does this insight offer freedom and grace in, to, (and possibly through) me?
4) What do I need to do in response to what God is saying to me?

4 - Lessons from the Cross

We have, of course, been learning lessons from the cross all of our Christian lives, but before we move on I do want to pause and think through a few of the practical ways we might seek to embed these lessons in our daily living. (In each of the three books in this series you will find a chapter like this one which is intended to be a kind of scatter-gun approach to stuff that might be helpful in your own devotional life. They are offered as seed-thoughts to prompt and resource you in your own praying and reflection. There are few right or wrong ways to interact with the various chapters of this book, of course, but it might be of interest to know what is in my mind as I write.)

I split my thinking into two basic chunks in this chapter. Firstly I offer a few quick fire thoughts, each of which may spark further reflection. They are the kind of thoughts that could be used to inform a day or a season of prayer, should you wish to use them in that way. Then, after offering a worked example from the Acts of the Apostles, I want to give a little more space to reflecting on what the cross of Christ says about the identity of the followers of Christ. Within this let me freely confess that this is not an exhaustive or authoritative study, it is simply what I notice as a long-time searcher of the Scriptures. I will trespass a little between the two types of ponderings, but I hope that you will forgive me for this. The other thing I find myself wanting to say to you, dear imagined reader, is that both matter. We need to be shaped by the story of scripture because we are narrative people: real people following a real God, in the real world, caught up in his infinitely bigger story. We need to begin to capture this in imagination and patterns which can be lived. We also, though, need to be able to wrestle this to the ground and summarise it in order that the rational mind might engage deeply with it. Don't lose either the fruits of detailed study or the shaping offered by wider reflection as you reflect on the Bible as both are gifts.

Some quick-fire daily insights from the cross

Each and every day of our Christian lives is lived in the light of the cross. In every season there will be insights which will be crucial to our discipleship and it is quite normal and good that these vary over time. Let me offer a few which regularly recur in my own praying, wrestling, or reflecting as I come back to kneel at the foot of the cross in my own devotions. Like you, I imagine, I do this in every season: in joy and in pain, in confusion, despair, confidence, and hope; the cross is that anchor point around which both our personal and our shared history pivots and in which it is held firm.

God really does love you more than you have yet realised

On the cross we glimpse the remarkable depth and breadth, the height and width of the love of God[43]. Indeed, John will explicitly argue that *'We know love by this, that he [Jesus] laid down his life for us[44]'.*

I often say in sermons that if I could teach the church one thing it would probably be to open people's eyes to the extraordinary manner in which they are loved. The love of God transforms everything: he is not manipulative, partial, fleeting, distractable, selfish, unkind, or flawed in any way. He is good, kind, attentive, persistent, wise, and never ever gives up on you. You are loved.

---

[43] I am deliberately echoing Ephesians 3.14-19 here which is, at least, informed by the cross and arguably is a reflection upon it.
[44] 1 John 3.16a NRSVA

This means that you are welcome

You are welcome because you are loved not because you are worthy. You are welcome the first time you come to Christ, and the thousandth time you come crawling back to him with your tail between your legs having messed things up all over again.

Just as the younger son comes to his senses in a far off land and heads home knowing that there will be a place for him[45], so you are invited, looked for, loved, and welcome. You do not need to beg, to pretend, to bribe your way in, or to make promises you cannot keep. You do not need to clean up your act first or become someone you are not. You just need to come home: you are welcome.

There is hope

I think this is one of the things that touches me most deeply about following Jesus. We are hope-people because he is a hope-giving saviour. There is no situation he cannot transform, renew, heal, or revive. Hope may well not be easy to birth, but it is always present and it is rooted on the hill called Golgotha outside Jerusalem two millennia ago.

I find myself returning again and again to the beginning of Ephesians 2 in my prayers. There is no hope at all in the first words, 'You were dead', and Paul does not duck this: he explains why we were dead and lost. I fear we move too quickly over them though. We were not merely afflicted, inconvenienced, wrong, or dispossessed. We had deceased. Life was gone. There was no hope and nothing in which hope could be grounded. We were 'children of wrath'.

But then comes verse 4, 'But God...' and we see life, forgiveness, risen hope[46].

There is always hope in Christ.

---

[45] See Luke 15.11-24 – see book 3 for an extended reflection on this parable.
[46] Verses taken from Ephesians 2.1-10 NRSVA

We do not need to understand

Please notice this: our hope does not depend upon our understanding, it depends entirely upon Jesus, and hope is opened up as we accept and cooperate with him. This is so important in our rationalistic materialist world where we quickly limit the goodness of God to the things that we can grasp. Let me get liturgical on you a moment and ask which of the dominical sacraments (ie the stuff Jesus told to do as he had done[47]) depend on our understanding for their efficacy? Do you imagine for a moment that someone who has an advanced degree in theology somehow receives more of Jesus than someone coming for the very first time to Holy Communion? Does the fact that Peter clearly had no idea what Jesus was doing when he washed his feet[48] diminish the power of Jesus' actions? This, as I will explore elsewhere in these books, is partly why I am cautious about some arguments concerning 'believer's baptism' as it is all too easy to suggest the validity of that sign of God's grace depends on the faith of the candidate rather than the grace of God.

You do not need to understand it in order to receive God's grace: you simply need to be placed into his hands and, in so far as you are able, accept that grace. The cross stamps this in your reality and mine.

God makes the first (and decisive) move

More broadly, we need to notice the repeated pattern in the Bible: it is God who makes the first move. This is explicit in places, for example when John unpacks the nature of love in his first letter and explains that 'we love because he first loved us[49]', but it is written throughout the narrative of the Scriptures. We

---

[47] Controversially, perhaps, or at least in a not-very-Anglican way, I tend to agree with the Orthodox Churches, that this is three things: Baptism, Holy Communion, and Foot Washing.
[48] See John 13.1-17
[49] 1 John 4.19

inhabit creation because we are first created, we are people of covenant because we are held in eternal covenant love, we come to repentance because we are taught and invited, and so on. Prophets are sent to those who are not yet listening, Christ is born into a world which is still in darkness, and the cross is raised by the very people who have the greatest need of the grace it will unlock.

There are so many truths to unpack here, but for me it often comes back to the simple realisation that as I pray something through I need to be alert to the fact that God is already on the case. I, indeed we, are not starting from scratch and God is not an unwilling participant.

Death is not the end

This could not be more obvious as we look at the cross, could it?

Again, we can take this in so many helpful directions (which I don't think I could ever fully unpack), but for me the most practical lesson is around the inclination of the heart. There is a profound shift in our approach to dying when we meet Christ, and this shapes all that we are. It shapes the end of this earthly life, of course, but it also shapes our daily living and we are wise to attend to this both personally and in community. The pattern of following Christ is a cross-carrying death and resurrection pattern. This is true in the practical stuff of daily living, but also true in ministry and fellowship. Death is still painful, hard, and can be difficult, but it is not the end.

Embracing crucifixion

There are so many more lines of thought that I hope this will spark in you, but the final one I will highlight for now is the central calling to be one who carries the cross rather than imposing the cost of it on others. Paul's language about having been crucified with Christ (and thus Christ living in and through his own life) is very powerful[50]. There is far more going on in this passage, theologically, than a call to bear the cost of mission with Christ and for others. However, one of the things that is here, and that we must not miss is precisely this point: the missioner bears the cost of the mission. We live as a crucified people, bearing, albeit in tiny part, the pain of the world around us. We don't do this as some kind of masochistic spirituality or heroic gesture. We don't do it to allow others to abuse us. We don't do it to wallow in grief or merely be a people of pain. We do it because this is the way life is. There is pain. There is disagreement. There is division and heartache and sin and brokenness. This can only ever be fully held by Christ on the cross, and then partially held by us: as we cling to Christ we cling to his crucifixion. The brokenness is not denied, parcelled off, or negated. As our fractured reality is embraced in prayer, in worship, in the indwelling of the Holy Spirit, the beginning of transformation begins to take place.

For me, personally, I note at least two implications for my own discipleship. I notice that, as I cling tighter to Christ, I also cling tighter to his crucifixion and this means that I cannot escape the harder parts of life or discipleship, and should not be surprised when it is painful. Also, though, when mission and service are painful and I find myself pushed into a place which feels like it has echoes of crucifixion to it: even here, I can seek Jesus in the midst of it all and I will discover that I am being pushed into the arms of Christ. These arms are already stretched wide and holding both the situation and me. This radically transforms my praying in the tougher places of ministry and life.

A worked biblical example

In a moment we will look at one larger lesson that we inhabit in the light of the cross, but firstly let me notice that these lessons

---

[50] See Galatians 2.19-21

are not ones that we, alone, need to learn. They are part of the life of the people of God throughout the ages, for we will always be a cruciform people if we are Christ's people.

Think of (or reread) the story of Peter and Cornelius in Acts 10, and ask yourself what you see happening. We see something like the following:

- Verses 1-2: We see Cornelius, a devout man but one who is a Gentile (outside the covenant) and a Roman soldier (an oppressive member of the occupying force).
- Verses 3-4: God sends an angel to meet Cornelius: he has heard, he is responding, and now Cornelius is clearly shown to be loved and welcomed by God.
- Verses 4-6: Where hope is impossible, God offers instructions that open a new possibility for Cornelius.
- Meanwhile, verses 9-16: God is already talking to Peter. God makes the first move (surprise, surprise).
- Verse 17: Peter does not understand at all (again, perhaps this is not a surprise).
- Verses 19 (where Peter is still pondering) – 29: Peter obeys even though he has been trained, by the whole weight of the rich inheritance of faith that has gone before, that this is stepping outside covenant. He bears the cost of doing as he is told, of choosing to go. He steps out in grace as he is instructed.
- Verses 34ff: old covenantal restrictions (to the Jewish people) come to an end. The church enters new territory, but in Christ this is not the end.

This pattern of a heart open to the Spirit of God, embracing the lost and marked by a willingness to go to them rather than expect them to come to us must surely be a key hallmark of the follower of Christ in every age.

An invitation to cruciform identity

I could go on, but I hope that these quick thoughts serve to get you pondering and praying as we seek to learn from the cross. What I plan to do now, though, is to reflect for a while on one deeper invitation from a number of angles. I wonder if the biggest problem that we have, assuming that we take the cross seriously, of course, is that we engage with it as if it were purely functional. We can so easily speak, think, preach, pray, and act as if the cross is a sort of legal or financial exchange: *"Tis done; the great transaction's done'*, to misuse Doddridge's great hymn.

Whilst there are many many actions, interactions, and transactions that take place at Calvary, the cross is far more than any one of them alone, or any combination of them. The cross defines who we are rather than simply prescribing what we do, it reveals and restores our fundamental identity not merely our tribe, allegiance, or understanding. This always matters for the people of God, but seems particularly apposite today when the key question around us today is not, I dare to suggest again, mainly about sexuality; it is chiefly about identity. Who am I? Whose am I?

The very core of our identity as Christians is not that we belong to (a) church, or a specific group of Christians. It is absolutely vital that we do, of course, for the church is the body of Christ. Putting the desires of the body above the invitation of God, though, will always lead to brokenness: and this is as true for the church as it is for the individual. The very core of our identity is that we are remade through the cross, that we belong to Christ, and we are called into the world.

We are redeemed missional people. We are washed and sent. We are made new and invited into the family business. We are reborn and set free. We are rescued, adopted, welcomed, and loved... and named ambassadors of this grace. We are invited, fed, teased, challenged, disciplined, enjoyed, and made part of the royal table-fellowship of the King of kings.

I have long been enthralled by Paul's description of the person, work, and nature of Christ in his letter to the church in Colossae where this is so profoundly held together:

> He [Jesus] is the image of the invisible God, the firstborn of all creation; for in him all things in heaven and on earth were created, things visible and invisible, whether thrones or dominions or rulers or powers—all things have been created through him and for him. He himself is before all things, and in him all things hold together. He is the head of the body, the church; he is the beginning, the firstborn from the dead, so that he might come to have first place in everything. For in him all the fullness of God was pleased to dwell, and through him God was pleased to reconcile to himself all things, whether on earth or in heaven, by making peace through the blood of his cross[51].

Here we glimpse the cross set in all the fulness of its biblical context, and I love the image of recreation worked at Calvary by the one who created us. It leads me to set the crucifixion alongside the creation narratives and reflect. Let's step back a moment and consider what it tells us about ourselves and our deepest identity.

We are created...

The cross only 'works' because of the fundamental link between creator and creation. As Paul explores in Colossians 1, Christ is creator which means that Christ can be redeemer. As we have just noted, this is possible because, *'in him all the fullness of God was pleased to dwell, and through him God was pleased to reconcile to himself all things, whether on earth or in heaven, by making peace through the blood of his cross.[52]'*

This glimpse into recreation opens our eyes afresh to creation. As we come to the cross, we are reminded that God created human beings in the beginning of all things[53]. He created us

---

[51] Colossians 1.15-20

[52] Colossians 1.19-20

[53] See Genesis 1.26ff, and Genesis 2.7ff

male and female, in his image, for each other, and placed us within the rest of creation to steward the earth. We might choose to do a variety of things with this foundational understanding of our humanity, but we need to recognise that this has long been our shared, Christian, foundation. It is descriptive, normative, and presented without expectation of controversy. As we reflect on the cross we are drawn back to our nature as created beings engaging with our creator. He does not intervene as an external consultant, technician, or meddling DIY-er: he intervenes as God recreating and making new. He intervenes in love and in so doing reminds us of who we are and who we are called to be.

... in the image of God...

Please notice from the two passages just referenced, both that *we* are created in the image of God and that *Jesus* is the image of the invisible God[54]. As Christ fully identifies with us so he can fully save us. On the cross we see our humanity hung before us and the redemptive grace of God raised before us. Here, in this holy place, we glimpse something of what it is to be in the image of God.

We see, for example, that being in the image of God is being by nature a servant bearing a deep call to serve. This is clearly set out in Philippians 2 which describes Jesus' attitude that led him to his cross, but it is also clear in the foundational creative purpose of humanity in stewarding creation and taking care of it[55]. This servant-nature of the faithful people of God is reflected throughout the Scriptures. A different illustration of this would be the images of Wisdom painted for us in the book of Proverbs. Proverbs is an ode to Wisdom which (who) is

---

[54] The word in Colossians 1.15 and the Septuagint (the Greek language version of the Old Testament which New Testament writers would have had access to) rendering of Genesis 1.26 is exact the same word, εἰκὼν or image.

[55] In Genesis 1.28-30 and Genesis 2.15 we see that God places humankind within creation (or the garden) to tend it, oversee it, manage it, and care for it.

represented throughout as a woman[56], not least by the capable wife of Proverbs 31.10-31. Wisdom is exemplary in many ways, for example in her industrious service, and the echoes of this resound in Christian teaching. Service is not merely a consequence of a protestant work ethic, it is part of our created rhythm and health: I chuckle each time I read 2 Thessalonians 3.6-13 and hear again Paul's blunt instruction to Christians to get off their backsides and contribute something useful to the cause, just as he seeks to. We are no mere recipients of heavenly beneficence as followers of Christ.

There are at least two further implications that we might note as we see humanity writ large on the cross. Firstly, and slightly paradoxically, we see that we are not alone. Christ's concern for John and his mother is profound[57] and reflects God's early (and, thus, axiomatic) observation, diagnosis, and statement that it is not good for man to be alone[58]. There are times when we can be tempted to interpret the cross individualistically (as if it merely enables my personal relationship with God), but this is never the full picture.

Secondly, notice that life in the image of God is fruitful. As we recall the narrative of creation alongside the narrative of crucifixion we see both the procreative intent of marital relations[59] set out with simple clarity and the salvific intent of crucifixion[60] with equal clarity. Humanity is created and blessed with the gift of passing on life.

---

[56] I like the fact that wisdom is represented as female, but am not sure that this is really a gendered point (any more than I think that God is male in a human sense even though male pronouns are used for him in the Bible).

[57] See John 19.26

[58] See Genesis 2.18, noting that this is not a gendered point (it is not good for women to be alone either).

[59] See Genesis 1.28

[60] See Colossians 2.13-15

... in relationship...

We have seen already that we are not alone, but need to take a step further and spot that the human identity embodied on the cross is one that is fundamentally relational. The restoration of creation that is achieved in part by Christ being forsaken[61] (and thus cut out of relationship) is not undertaken merely so we might have company, it is established for relationship. We have noted the establishment of new familial relationship around the cross, and this echoes both with the creation narratives where Adam and Eve are literally made for each other, and with the wider flow of the Bible. Relationality spans the metanarrative and constantly reappears in the drama of the Scriptures. Genealogy matters throughout, not merely in the overlooked passages at the beginning of two of the four gospels. The story of the people of God is that of marriage and lineage. Israel herself is seen as a child by Hosea. The Church is described many times as the bride of Christ[62]. The apostle Paul likens Christ's relationship with the church to that of husband to wife. In the middle of the Bible we find the Song, often attributed to Solomon. Preachers often don't really know what to do with the text as it is a bit fruity in its description of intimate, sexual, love between a young woman and young man. It is explicit, rampant, joyful, unashamed, and deeply bodily.

Most clearly in the descriptions of the eschaton, Christ returns as a bride-groom, with the Church as the waiting bride. We see this in the Revelation of St John the Divine, not least as we hear that great final invitation as the *'Spirit and the Bride say "Come!"[63]'*. We see it in the parables of Christ as he speaks of

---

[61] See Mark 15.33
[62] For example, Ephesians 5.25-32 explores this metaphor.
[63] Revelation 22.7

the wise and the foolish bridesmaids[64], or the coming bridegroom[65].

We are relational beings, and we need to note in today's climate that this does not only mean we are sexual beings. Indeed, we should never present an exclusively sexual, or an overly perfect picture of relationships in the Bible. Our identity as it is described in the Bible, whilst relational, is very far from predominantly or definitively sexual. Without being indelicate, never forget that the Christ who died on the cross died as a virgin also died as one who had evidenced the most remarkable relationships with others. Deep, intimate, life-giving and non-sexual friendship abounds. Jesus and his disciples, the travelling apostles, David and Jonathan, Elijah and Elisha, Naomi and Ruth, or the companies of the prophets all bear testimony to this.

Furthermore, the Bible is littered with stories of redeemed misdirected intimacy, from the polygamous relationships of the Patriarchs to the fact that our Lord is descended from Bathsheba. Which of us doesn't wince when we read of Rachel and Leah simply giving their servants Bilhah and Ziphah to Jacob their husband in order to bear them children? *"Here is Bilhah, my servant. Sleep with her so that she can bear children for me and I too can build a family through her.[66]"* How can it be that the union of David and Bethsheba, founded as it is on murder, adultery, and polygamy, gives rise to the birth of the saviour of humanity? We are rooted in grace that ranges far beyond our understanding, and is not limited to our expectation or even hope.

... fallen...

And here reality bites, for both the creation narrative and the crucifixion point with unwavering determination to the reality

---

[64] Matthew 25.1-12
[65] This image is in a number of places, I am thinking here of Matthew 9.15 .
[66] Genesis 30^3

of our brokenness before God. However you read Genesis 3.1-6, you cannot escape the diagnosis that the will of God differs from the choices made by humanity and that this is deeply problematic. The fear that we see (humanity's fear of God and by implication of each other) in Genesis 3.7-8 is merely the first sign of the problems that result. We might get our modern theological knickers in a twist about the concept of sin, but without some understanding of this fundamental dislocation between humanity and God, we cannot understand either the Bible or the Gospel.

Each and every time we see God engaging with humanity we see this recognition of the need to reshape our lives according to his will and way. There are times when the frustration at our unwillingness to hear and respond is almost palpable in the text. Look at the prophets if you don't believe me! Take Amos for example: Amos 3.6-13 paints a vivid picture of God's repeated attempts to correct and heal his people and their complete refusal to hear and respond. At times this comes across in judgement, but often (perhaps usually), there is also a hopeful heartbeat accompanying the warnings. The Lord is like a refiner's fire or fuller's soap, says Malachi[67], fully cognisant of our imperfection compared to God's glorious majesty but at the same time holding out the hope of cleansing that runs like a heartbeat throughout the Bible.

... but loved, invited, and transformed...

On the cross, as we gaze on the very heart of our identity, we see not only the reality of the consequences of our sin, but also the astonishing dawn of hope in the most unlikely of places. On the cross, the proffered forgiveness and hope is manifestly offered, indeed it is paradoxically enabled, only within the very brokenness it is uniquely able to address.

The story of the Bible is no escapist perfectionism where a nice God meets nice people and does nice things with and for them.

---

[67] See Malachi 3.1-4

Nor, at its core is it some kind of magic salvation offered from beyond our current situation, inviting escape from this life into some early or easy paradise. Early on in faith, particularly in the way that 'Bible Stories' are told to children, it might look like this is the way the text will lead us. Noah is spared from the flood because he is a righteous man[68]. Joseph wins great reward because he refuses to break God's rules, even if he is a tad gauche and alienates his brothers[69]. Job is picked on because he is set up as a paradigm in the heavens[70]. Daniel and his fiery chums are set apart and set upon because they are boldly holy[71]. Jeremiah gets thrown in a sewer[72], but is still faithful. Even Jonah, who gets it wrong to start with, gets to swim with the dolphins and lead the most remarkable 3-day evangelistic crusade in the history of the planet[73].

This is not the full picture, though; far from it, in fact. It overlooks Abraham's choice of Hagar to manipulate God's promise[74], Moses' murderous activity[75], David's adultery[76], Peter's denial[77], and Paul's self-confessed ongoing wrestling with 'the things he does not want to do[78]'. All of these broken acts of broken people play a role in the unfolding narrative of God's work of salvation in the world. We may not fully understand them (I certainly don't), but they matter and are part of the flow of scriptural grace.

---

[68] See Genesis 6.9, or Hebrews 11.7

[69] See Genesis 37 and following chapters.

[70] Note that in Job 1.8 it is God Himself who holds Job up as an example of righteousness.

[71] I am thinking particularly of Daniel being thrown into the Lion's Den in Daniel 6, or of Shadrach, Meshach and Abednego being cast into the fiery furnace as we see in Daniel 3.

[72] Jeremiah 38

[73] The reference here is just the book of Jonah – and yes, I know that we usually talk of a whale, but the text simply says a big fish.

[74] Genesis 16.1-4ff

[75] Exodus 2.11

[76] 2 Samuel 11

[77] Luke 24.54-62

[78] c.f. Romans 7.19 for example.

Most clearly, though, we hold the cross of Christ in front of us. Here is the crucial centre of God's atoning work. Here the worship of the first covenant is completed and rendered unnecessary as the One Lamb is offered in eternally efficacious atoning sacrifice for all people everywhere and everywhen. Here the blood-price of redemption is paid in full. Here death is defeated in death itself. Here we see encapsulated the mystery of God's loving purposes in and for humanity in multi-layered and inexhaustible complexity which is unfailingly simple. Jesus dies so we might live; in his wretched murder hope is restored and love rises triumphant...

... and this is only possible because the very brokenness that needed so desperately to be healed, transformed, forgiven, and crucified itself crucifies the only one who can offer the salvation it needs. Salvation is only made possible as the very sinfulness from which we need to be saved pins the saviour to the cross. Christ defeats death only as death grasps hold of him.

... as sin and death and hell are defeated

Here is an extraordinary mysterious truth. If humankind had welcomed Jesus and not nailed him to a cross, how would our salvation have been won? If we had greeted the Messiah with indifference or middle-class politeness, if we had ignored Jesus and simply sidelined his views until he went away, he would not have become the sacrificial lamb necessary for the salvation of the very ones who turned on him.

This is mind-blowing!

At least, I find it mind-blowing: God's primary act of salvation not only redeems the sinfulness of creation, the very methodology of redemption depends on the very sin that it has come to defeat.

This is the extent of the redemption of God!

Salvation from sin is only won (this is crystal clear in the Biblical narrative) in the midst of sin and only made effective by the sinful action of those needing salvation.

This insight is so important. Truly Christian good news does not tell of an 'external' god who invades our world and tells of a different reality to which we can escape if we follow his secret way. The Christ-story is of a broken-hearted holy Creator who sees that calling out to his people does not transform the heart, either of the person or of the problem, and thus chooses to step into his own creation and redeem it from the inside out, allowing the very brokenness which has corrupted all to be the weapon which breaks the deadlock and unlocks recreation.

Of course he will recreate the heavens and the earth, and we look forward to the time we stand with him beyond our current reality, but the path there is not escapism, it is redemption. Christianity speaks of the God who transforms from the inside out, redeeming, renewing, restoring, and recreating.

Salvation is found in the midst of brokenness, not by running away from it. Do you want to find Christ? Go and search among the sinners! He came to seek and to save the lost, not to minister to the already-perfect (or those who think themselves already perfect). It is not the healthy who need a doctor, after all, but the sick[79], and Jesus was known as the one who hung out with prostitutes and tax-collectors.

Hope, or at least Christian hope, is found in the midst of sin. New beginnings start, with Christ, where people are not where others might like them to be or where they might pretend to be. Redemption is, therefore, possible, and it is possible for all. In Jesus' crucifixion we see God's work of atonement enacted and enabled at heart of sinful creation: here is hope and it is to be found among sinners.

---

[79] Cf Luke 5.31

This cross-shaped identity and inheritance, my dear unseen reading companions, is both who we are and who we are called to be. Never lose sight of the cross, and never lose sight of this invitation to hope birthed in the deepest darkness and the most profound despair, for here is life and life in all its fulness[80].

---

[80] See John 10.10, in which both the threat and the promise we have been exploring are held together.

4A – PAUSING FOR BREATH

Pause for a moment and consider...

What issues are you wrestling with that have caused you to pick up this book?

If the following questions are useful, please use them to reflect:

1) What have I noticed the Spirit of saying to me in this chapter?
    a) What have I learned?
    b) Where do I want to reflect further?
    c) What ideas will not go away?
2) How is Jesus shaping, moulding, or redefining your identity as you read?
3) What hope do I glimpse here?
4) What do I need to do in response to what God is saying to me?

5 - THE CROSS: HOW THEN DO WE LIVE?

Were you there when they crucified my Lord?
Were you there when they crucified my Lord?
While sometimes it causes me to tremble, tremble, tremble
Were you there when they crucified my Lord?

And here, I pause... does the cross cause me to wonder, to tremble, to reflect... even, actually, to pause?

Really?

It is easy to see how others can pass by the cross without seeing what is happening, but what of me? The old saying 'familiarity breeds contempt' can be true even of the most holy and central parts of our lives. How am I to live? To see? To be cross-shaped and cross-motivated? If we are serious about walking the way of the cross, how do we actually live in its light? How do we take up our cross and follow[81]? What does it look like to live in a cross-shaped way today?

There are, of course, so many answers to that, and these books set out to explore some of them. You will find a chapter like this in each of the three books, and in some (perhaps in many) ways these sections are interchangeable because gospel life hangs together as a whole and is really only broken down in the consideration; it is lived as a whole. I will try to make the links below, but the three 'headlines' that shape these reflections hang together: unity, mission, and worship. Our unity is missional (as Jesus prays, for example, in John 17) as is our worship. As we engage in mission, we discover that we need to

---

[81] Matthew 14.24

stand together (think of foodbanks, for example), and worship naturally arises.

Whilst each response could be put where the others are, there is a logic at least in my mind. We will ponder a number of things (including holiness, unity, character, worship, and mission) but we start with mission because it seems to me that this is the great invitation of God. You and I are called to come, not only to be made new, but to discover what it is to join our Lord in the greatest of all his works, the work of loving rescue, redemption, and hope. This gift of life is the central gift that was not previously possible, but has now been brought into living reality in the cross. We are held together as one with each other and with God, how can we not seek to draw others into the place of reconciliation?

We who are faithful are always called to a worshipful, unified, infectious, ongoing, persistent outward orientation in mission.

What do I mean by mission?

I realise, though, that I am using a term in a certain way and I need to be clear what I am talking about if we are to communicate well. The word 'mission' simply comes from a Latin word meaning 'being sent' (just like the word 'apostle', which comes from the Greek word for 'being sent'). In Christian circles we take for granted that it is God who is doing the sending, and that he is doing so in order to carry forward the work that Christ came to achieve. A very significant part of this was achieved on the cross. We have already discussed the need to remember that Christ did other important things too, but arguably the cross is the key that unlocks them all.

Christ came to reveal God in all God's amazing goodness, as well as to bridge the chasm between us. As Paul puts it, he is the visible image of the invisible God: he made all things, holds all things together, and reconciles to himself all things[82].

Why are we sent? Look at Matthew 28: we are sent to make disciples of all nations. This will involve evangelism (explaining the good news of Jesus to people and giving them a chance to respond), but will often start a long way before that with people who cannot grasp that God might even be real, let alone interested in them. Mission is sharing all goodness of God as we have experienced it in Christ. It is the stumbling effort that we make to share a love that is way beyond us. It is multi-faceted, relational, complicated, and yet utterly simple. We glimpse something of its breadth in the Anglican Communion's Five Marks of Mission[83], although it goes beyond even this breadth.

> The mission of the Church is the mission of Christ
> 1.   To proclaim the Good News of the Kingdom
> 2.   To teach, baptise and nurture new believers
> 3.   To respond to human need by loving service
> 4.   To transform unjust structures of society, to challenge violence of every kind and pursue peace and reconciliation
> 5.   To strive to safeguard the integrity of creation, and sustain and renew the life of the earth

Jesus' priorities

Jesus was very clear what he had come for and why. Let me remind you of a few, very familiar, Bible verses:

> For God so loved the world that he gave his only Son, so that everyone who believes in him may not perish but may have eternal life. Indeed, God did not send the Son into the world to condemn the world, but in order that the world might be saved through him.[84]

---

[82] See Colossians 1.15-20
[83] See little-house-in-joppa.uk/S&F202331 for link to online version
[84] John 3.16-17 NRSVA

> *'The Spirit of the Lord is upon me, because he has anointed me to bring good news to the poor.*
>
> *He has sent me to proclaim release to the captives and recovery of sight to the blind, to let the oppressed go free, to proclaim the year of the Lord's favour.'* [85]

> *Then Jesus said to him [Zacchaeus], 'Today salvation has come to this house, because he too is a son of Abraham. For the Son of Man came to seek out and to save the lost.'* [86]

> *I came that they may have life, and have it abundantly.* [87]

This is just the start of the examples we could give, for there is a very consistent theme throughout the gospels. Jesus came for the purpose of reconciliation between humanity (indeed, the whole of creation if you look at Paul's writing[88]) and God, he came to save, he came to seek the lost and bring them home.

The reckless shepherd

In another place, Jesus told this story about a farmer who had 100 sheep. If you have heard me preach about this you will know that I play with it because I can never quite get the story right when I retell it. Doesn't it go something like this:

> *And Jesus spake this parable unto them, saying, What man of you, having an hundred sheep, if he shalt lose ninety nine of them, doth not take an extra care of the remaining one and leave the ninety and nine in the wilderness, trusting that that which is lost might hearken unto the happy sound of the sole contented beast and in returning hithertofore of their true and wholesome volition be found? And all those he hath, even be it only one that dost not wander thence, he layeth on his*

---

[85] Luke 4.18-19 NRSVA

[86] Luke 19-9-10 NRSVA

[87] John 10.10b NRSVA

[88] Read Romans 8.19ff, for example

> shoulders nigh his own breast, rejoicing for with them he is
> truly shepherd.[89]

How can the story be any different? Only a fool would leave 99
sheep alone in the wilderness, for when he returned he would
find most of them scattered, killed, or lost. And yet...

... and yet in the way Jesus actually tells it, this is a story about
an idiot shepherd who is foolishly devoted to one lost sheep
who should really be written off.

> 'Which one of you, having a hundred sheep and losing one of
> them, does not leave the ninety-nine in the wilderness and go
> after the one that is lost until he finds it? When he has found
> it, he lays it on his shoulders and rejoices. And when he comes
> home, he calls together his friends and neighbours, saying to
> them, "Rejoice with me, for I have found my sheep that was
> lost."[90]

The answer to Jesus' question, 'which of you...' should be '*None
of us would, this is utter madness*'! But this is a story about a
God who refuses to do what even an idiot shepherd knows
must be done, because he will not let go of the wilful, obstinate,
disobedient, senseless sheep who has chosen his own path.
God's whole orientation is towards the lost. What did the Son
of Man come for? To seek and to save the lost. Who is it who
needs a doctor? It is not those who are well!

I love being part of the church (or at least I mostly love being
part of the church) but we are really not very good at this. On
every measure I can think of, our interest is very skewed
towards ourselves. Look at the agendas of our church councils,
synods, or meetings. Listen to the sermons which are offered.
Trace how we spend our money. Look at where we spend our
free time. Listen to the way we pray. It's not that we never

---

[89] You can compare this with Luke 15.3-6 for the real parable which we explore
here more fully. This 'version' is based on the King James Version for added
comic authenticity.
[90] Luke 15.4-6 NRSVA

focus any of this on the lost, but I fear the ratio might be close to 99:1... in the wrong direction!

A modern example

It is a long while since I read Vincent Donovan's seminal work 'Christianity Rediscovered', but it comes to mind almost every day. Here was a Catholic missionary priest sent to live among the Maasai who saw that the onus for mission truly was his. How would he communicate the timeless truth he had received in a manner which allowed this new people (from his perspective) to hear the truth that he had understood in a completely different culture? Somehow the drama is increased for me by the fact that he is Roman Catholic, but could not communicate with those in authority about what he was doing. This is not a congregationalist who would have been equipped to improvise depending on local context... and yet he was driven to establish church in a context which was as yet unknown to the Church. There were no adult Maasai Christians, and yet Vincent Donovan knew himself to be called. He describes very powerfully his conversations within the church and with his superiors. In particular he reflects on the call to do the work of mission by simply living among those to whom he was called and allowing the Good News to take root in that context.

He settles in the deep conviction that a missionary needs to respect the culture of those to whom he (or she) is sent, rather than replacing it. This changes the presentation of the gospel in astonishing ways; the gospel expands to become as significant a cultural foundation among those who receive it as the one it first encountered was. Equally, he then sets out how this transforms and enlivens his own inhabiting of the gospel.

Read it for yourself; it is deeply moving to see how this faithful priest rediscovers his own faith in the context of reaching an unreached people group. I confess that I think we live in something of a similar context now, and I love this text because it is one of the few that really wrestles with how we do mission when we live in exile. We are utterly addicted to doing mission as host; inviting others into what we have. Yet this is not the world in which we now live. We are guest. We are alien and stranger. We are visitor. We receive hospitality, and in so doing not only walk in the footsteps of the great missionary saints of old, we walk in the footsteps of Christ himself. Perhaps this is the biggest single missional challenge for the church today: how do we do mission as guest? Subverting. Transforming from the inside. Taking no spare cloak, tunic, cash, or sandals.

> For I decided to know nothing among you except Jesus Christ, and him crucified. And I came to you in weakness and in fear and in much trembling[91].

Our priorities?

This cuts to the heart of what really matters to us, and what comprises the very core of who we are. And, let's be brutally honest, whether we are willing to face up to what obstructs others hearing this? We must pause and reflect deeply, honestly, and regularly if we are to be faithful.

You might disagree with this, but I am convinced that the church has almost completely lost the culture war: society no longer agrees with us simply because we say something, if, indeed, it ever did. It might be worth considering whether such a culture war was the right thing to wage in the first place, as there are many lessons we can learn, but this is where we are now. In fact, of course, many others do agree with us about a whole lot of stuff and are looking for us to go into bat about all manner of issues because our voice is valued, but they do not give us the absolute authority that we seem to act as if we should have when it comes to questions of morality.

We might be conscious about this dynamic in the area of sexuality, but this is far from the only example we could call on;

---

[91] 1 Corinthians 2.2-3 NRSVA

we think differently about money, about international welfare, about sanctuary for asylum seekers, about the human body, about lotteries, to name but a few, and, of course, in each of these areas there is not simply one 'church view'. We think differently to those without faith, but we also think differently to each other (which is partly why I am cautious about waging culture war). We, as Christians, have huge riches to bring to these conversations, but perhaps they are less in the area of authoritative command (you must do this), and more around the question of how we engage, listen, prioritise, and decide[92]. The spaciousness of the cross sets the tone for our engagement with each other and with those who are beyond our circles of friendship, familiarity, or preference.

We have great resources in terms of specific insights (and I don't mean to diminish them by widening the spotlight in this way), but also methods of having difficult conversations, and there is a real appetite for us to offer these. Yet, I fear, we not only lose sight of the gifts with which we have been entrusted, we obsess about stuff that the outside world just thinks to be an irrelevance, and no matter how important we might think it is, the blunt truth is that if people are not interested they will not engage. The other day, I was talking to a very able church leader who is doing an amazing job growing a church in the toughest of areas, and he was tearing his hair out about some of the stuff that he needs to do as part of the Church of England: *we simply don't realise the enormity of our own irrelevance'*, he said in frustration...

... and I have to say; as I walked back to my car through a bustling modern Northern city-centre, I could not forget his words. The way we are, the things we argue about, much of our daily activity is simply irrelevant to those I walked past. We could not have a more urgent, vital, or apposite message but we do a very good job of hiding it.

---

[92] As a footnote, let me say that this is what I have appreciated about the Church of England's 'Living in Love and Faith' programme.

Who pays the cost of mission?

One of the most striking things about the cross is that God not only takes the initiative, he also bears the entire cost. It was whilst we were *dead* in our sins (and the uncircumcision of our flesh) that God made us alive in Christ[93]. Not only were we (almost certainly) unwilling to pay the cost, and (certainly) unable to pay the cost, we were not even alive to do it! If we look at things from the perspective of those outside the church, I wonder what we see. Might it be that we, albeit unwittingly, expect them to pay the cost of crossing our threshold[94]. Christ made himself nothing and came to us in our world[95]. Could it seem to others that his followers make ourselves holy and demand that others come out of their world before they might be part of what Christ has done?

When it comes to areas about which we feel strongly, be that social justice, climate change, sexuality, gender, identity, or any number of other issues: we as church face a choice. Will we pull up the drawbridge and wait for people to plead for entry into an institution they believe to be irrelevant at best and hate-ridden at worst, or let down the drawbridge and take the risk of living among those to whom we were sent? People often turn out to quite like individual Christians, and even specific groups of Christians, even in the instances where they loathe the institution. (It actually seems to me, this loathing is less predictable in either direction than we think it will be: I am constantly surprised by people feeling differently about the church to the way I think they will). This choice brings us back

---

[93] See Colossians 2.13, and don't worry too much about the 'uncircumcision of the flesh' bit. I include it so as not to redact the biblical text, but his is mainly just another reference to how far we are from God's way before Christ rescues us and makes sense in the context of the letter.

[94] I don't think we even realise it is a cost. When I used to train lay ministers in mission, we got them to visit a betting shop to place a bet (I don't think the idea was original to me) and then discuss how it felt. It was eye-opening to them to see how threatening and scary an alien environment is. The church is just the same for those who don't (yet) feel they belong there.

[95] See Philippians 2.

to our core beliefs and our deepest calling. At the risk of creating a false dichotomy: are we a frightened people whose fear that holiness might not work in the 'real world'? Or a missionary people whose main call is witness? A people who need to be on our guard lest we are polluted, or those carrying light into the darkness? Those under attack from powers beyond our understanding, or those in whom abides a greater One than he who is in the world?

This is a false polarity, of course, because we do need to be on our guard and to take care not to be polluted by the world[96], but the very fact that James needs to warn us of this assumes that we are living in the world. It's a little like taking a child on holiday from the UK to a country in which there are diseases not prevalent in the West. Only a foolish parent would fail to take the child for the advised inoculations. Only the most careless or ignorant would not instruct the child on the importance of washing hands, or of drinking only bottled or boiled water, and not stroking animals. However, the intention is not that the child stay in some Western complex in the heart of a foreign culture. The precautions are precisely so that the child can experience, engage, enjoy, and interact with the culture which is all around. Precaution is simply a matter of wise living, not a restriction on what can or should be done. And so it is, I would argue, with the New Testament except that we are here as exiles not merely as tourists, as salt and light not photographers or commentators. We are not called out of the world, we are instructed to live with wisdom and grace within it in order that the Good News might be heard.

In truth, if others pay the cost of our mission then we are not really taking up the cross and following; indeed, it seems to me that we are in grave danger of abandoning Christ's mission in favour of our own. Think about this another way: cast your mind back to the New Testament, and ask yourself about the

---

[96] See James 1.27, for example.

grounds on which you remember people being judged or condemned.

Matthew 24 and 25 might well come to mind. At the end of chapter 24 and beginning of 25 we have three mini-parables about being watchful and ready for the return of Christ. These often tie in, at least in my mind, with Matthew 7 where Jesus says *'Not everyone who says to me, 'Lord, Lord,' will enter the kingdom of heaven, but only the one who does the will of my Father who is in heaven.'*[97] As if he anticipates the response that people will give about the way that they have engaged in all sorts of activities which are clearly inspired by his life and work, he goes straight on: *'Many will say to me on that day, 'Lord, Lord, did we not prophesy in your name and in your name drive out demons and in your name perform many miracles?' Then I will tell them plainly, 'I never knew you. Away from me, you evildoers!'*[98]. This is not about works, or even about miraculous acts; it is about deep conversion of the heart. It is set in the context of the Sermon on the Mount, which is Jesus teaching on how we live holy and Godly lives. In Matthew 7 alone, we hear instruction about not judging others, about faithful trusting prayer, about disciplined followership, about building our lives on the rock-like foundation of Christ's word rather than the sandy foundation of this world's wisdom, and we are given the simple test by which we are to judge the teaching of others: look at the fruit they bear.

What about holiness?

Let's pause for a moment here, though, because these verses raise a vital matter. Which is our primary responsibility before God: holiness or mission? Am I arguing that we do not need to be holy because we must be missional?

---

[97] Matthew 7.21 NRSVA
[98] Matthew 7.22-23 NRSVA

Far from it! If that is what you take from my writing, then I wish I had never put finger to keyboard. Holiness matters! It matters deeply, profoundly, and eternally.

Holiness is, though, never separated from our missional task for to do so is to miss the entire point of holiness. Holiness is the setting apart of oneself for the purpose of honouring, glorifying, worshipping, and obeying the loving God. Holiness reflects the nature of God, and our God is a seeking and restoring God. Why did the Son of Man come? To seek and to save the lost! Seeking holiness without engaging in mission is little more than spiritual self-pleasuring; it is fruitless self-deception in the highest degree. Anyone can pretend to perfection if they are not willing to test the balsa-wood edifice of their finely crafted spirituality in robust interaction with the reality of the lives of those around them, but this is not really the path of wisdom or holiness. Real holiness rarely has clean fingernails or shiny paintwork. It is bruised, scratched, and bearing the marks of those it serves, and we glimpse it in the lives of those we admire most.

> But woe to you who are rich,
> for you have received your consolation.
> Woe to you who are full now,
> for you will be hungry.
> Woe to you who are laughing now,
> for you will mourn and weep.
> Woe to you when all speak well of you,
> for that is what their ancestors did to the false prophets.[99]

We return throughout these books to the question of holiness[100], as it really is key, but this question is really about the fundamental nature of our faith. Faith that only engages part of our lives or only survives in a vacuum is no real faith. Jesus calls us to a whole-life transformation which is infinitely more radical, risky, and real than this, and of which true holiness is the characteristic scent, 'feel', or mood. Holiness is

---

[99] Luke 6.24-26 NRSVA
[100] See chapter5 in books 2 and 3, both of which consider this further.

core to mission not because it denotes the bar over which people need to be able to hop before they can enter, but because it is the mouth-watering smell of baking bread that draws the hungry with salivating desire. It is the echoing music and laughing dancers that starts by getting feet tapping and ends up with the stranger drawn into the party.

The centrality of faith

Notice that passage from Luke that I just quoted. Is this about material wealth and poverty? In part it is, and we know this because we find the text in Luke's gospel and this is one of his recurring themes, but it is also around apparent spiritual wealth and poverty. Jesus seems to be speaking with the same tone the Apostle will adopt when deriding the Corinthian church[101] who think they have made it and have missed the point. Listen to what Jesus goes on to say in Luke 6:

> But I say to you that listen, Love your enemies, do good to those who hate you, bless those who curse you, pray for those who abuse you. If anyone strikes you on the cheek, offer the other also; and from anyone who takes away your coat do not withhold even your shirt. Give to everyone who begs from you; and if anyone takes away your goods, do not ask for them again. Do to others as you would have them do to you.[102]

Spiritual wealth, and the blessing of God, rests in the way we engage with the 'outsider', and particularly those in need. Consider the sheep and goats in Matthew 25. The passage ends with the separation of the sheep and the goats on the last day when all are judged with the 'sheep' being welcomed as the King says 'Come, you that are blessed by my Father, inherit the kingdom prepared for you from the foundation of the world' [103] The 'goats', in the 1st century, would have been almost indistinguishable from from sheep and are sent packing: 'You

---

[101] See 1 Corinthians 4.8, for example.
[102] Luke 6.27-31 NRSVA
[103] Matthew 25.34 NRSVA

that are accursed, depart from me into the eternal fire prepared for the devil and his angels[104]'

What is it that separates them? In each case it is the way that they have treated Christ when he presented himself as the needy stranger; *'for I was hungry and you gave me food, I was thirsty and you gave me something to drink, I was a stranger and you welcomed me, I was naked and you gave me clothing, I was sick and you took care of me, I was in prison and you visited me.[105]',* or in the goats' case, you failed to do any of these. *'"Truly I tell you, just as you did not do it to one of the least of these, you did not do it to me." And these will go away into eternal punishment, but the righteous into eternal life.[106]'*

This is social gospel teaching, but it is more than this; it reflects the profoundly missional heart of God. This is about real clothes, actual food, costly care, and personal fellowship, but it is also about reaching out with the riches of the Kingdom Christ came to establish. We can see this if we attend to the chunk in the middle of Matthew 25 missing from my earlier trot through of the chapter. Right in the middle we find the parable of the talents, which often seems misplaced to me, sitting, as it does, sandwiched within this chapter. It also seems strangely meritocratic in the manner it is usually taught: almost as if it is saying, *'look, even Jesus teaches that you are to do your best with the gifts you have been given!'* I associate it with school assembly and parents encouraging children to work hard and enjoy what life will give. Both of these misunderstandings, though, arise from our wrenching of the parable out of its context and as all who engage with the Bible ought to know, this is dangerous: *a text without a context is a pretext for a proof text!*

You know the story: a master goes away leaving his wealth with 3 servants and trusts them to care for all that is his. One invests

---

[104] Matthew 25.41 NRSVA
[105] Matthew 25.35-36 NRSVA
[106] Matthew 25.45b-46 NRSVA

his 5 talents, and how confusing that we still use that word as it means 'ability' to us (this is an example, I think, of really misleading translation). A talent was 60 minas, a mina was 50 shekels, a shekel was 2 bekas, and a beka was 10 gerahs. So, the first invests his 300,000 gerahs, or 375lbs, or 175kg, or (assuming this was gold) over £6m, or 75 years of wages... anyway, the point is that the bloke invests huge wealth, not his ability, on behalf of the master, and doubles the money. The second does the same with a mere £2.5m and doubles that, and the one we think of as poor as he is only entrusted with £1.2m goes and sticks it in a hole in the ground; behind closed doors, in a place no-one would think to look for it so that it is undefiled and safe. When the master returns he is delighted with the 5-guy and the 2-guy but furious with the 1-guy.

As I say, we hear this as being about a waste of talent (in the modern sense), or about laziness, or about a failure to make profit, but listen to what the master actually says: *'You knew, did you, that I reap where I did not sow, and gather where I did not scatter?*[107]*'* These words are written in the gospel of Matthew. How can they not remind us of the parable of the sower[108]? There it is completely clear that the task is sharing the word of Jesus. And think about where this parable is situated in the gospel: it is sandwiched between ten bridesmaids and the mixed flock of sheep and goats. This is not a story for adolescents who need to be motivated to do something with life; it is a heart cry into mission. What is the greatest treasure we have been given? It is the Good News. Invest it! Share it! Risk it! Don't, for heaven's sake, stick it in a place where no-one will ever look for it out of fear that it will be lost.

Faith is to be risked in public, not hidden in private. Like money, it will grow, and if you are not sure, at least put it in the bank! You are the missional, outward looking, kingdom-building,

---

[107] Matthew 25.26 NRSVA
[108] See Matthew 25.1-23

disciple-making, stranger-feeding, prisoner-visiting people of God! Live it out. Live it outside.

And, lest you are still unconvinced, look at where Luke places the parallel parable. The same story, with minor changes, follows Jesus bringing salvation to the house of Zacchaeus the hated tax collector[109], and precedes him entering Jerusalem as the promised Messianic King[110].

The centrality of mission

I could go on, but I don't think I need to. The point I am making is simple and clear; it is true that judgement day is coming and we will be judged on the holiness of our lives, but this is far from a simple question of moral purity. Judgement is focussed in the New Testament on those who have lost sight of the missional purposes of God, who have let go of the great commission with which our Lord left us:

> All authority in heaven and on earth has been given to me. Go therefore and make disciples of all nations, baptizing them in the name of the Father and of the Son and of the Holy Spirit, and teaching them to obey everything that I have commanded you. And remember, I am with you always, to the end of the age[111].

Indeed (and with this I will draw this particular line of thought to a close) one of the very first 'fruits' of humanity's rebellion against God in the opening chapters of the Bible, after Cain has murdered his brother Abel, is his retort to God that he is not his brother's keeper[112]. I love the former Archbishop of York, Archbishop Sentamu's indignant observation about this; you are not called to be your brother's keeper, you are called to be your brother's brother! Faith in the God and Father of our Lord Jesus Christ is always outward looking, missional, generous,

---

[109] Luke 19.1-10
[110] Luke 19vv28ff
[111] Matthew 28.18-20 NRSVA
[112] Genesis 4.9

and expansive... because he is always more outward looking, missional, generous, and expansive than we can imagine.

This is to be the first and most visible of the faithful Christian's 'holy habits' or 'spiritual disciplines'. Just as Jesus did as he saw the Father doing[113], so we are called to do as he does. We only need to take it one manageable step at a time, but it is a journey we must take, deliberate step by deliberate step.

The privilege of mission

I fear, though, that if we stopped at this point, we would be in danger of falling into another apparent lurking trap of our modern missional thinking, where we almost seem to think that mission is a kind of unpleasant duty to which we need to attend. Sometimes it seems as if we feel that mission is like the spiritual equivalent of cleaning the loo: unpleasant, necessary, if we just get on with it we will hardly notice the chore, but secretly we hope that someone else will do it.

This could not be further from the case, and it certainly could not be further from the tone that the Bible seems to want to set. I guess there are times when we all need to be jolted into action around things that are important, but I don't think that God wants to make you feel guilty enough to get out and share your faith: the question is why on earth you would not want to. The greatest privilege in the world is to participate in the work that God is doing. Surely the lasting tragedy of the story of the two sons in Luke 15 is not that the younger one runs away, but that the older one distances himself from his father's work when he sees the younger welcomed home. He is at home but chooses not to belong, not to participate, not to celebrate, not to embrace or inhabit his identity as beloved child, welcomed brother, part of the father's family. This parable is key, not only for the teaching it offers, but also for the context it sets. If you

---

[113] See John 5.19

want to balance the task we have been given with the freedom that comes with the gospel it seems to me that the context of loving relationship is exactly the place to hold this tension. If I love you, there are all manner of things that I will choose to do for you. I may have to do them, I might choose to do so, but the distinction is far less costly and far more human than merely acting under compulsion.

Cross-carrying, you see, will cost you everything. There is nothing harder, more demanding, more sacrificial. Yet at the same time, there is nothing more liberating, more exciting, more adventurous. It is, as one of the great prayers at communion puts it, both a duty and a joy. This is our responsibility, but it is also our privilege. This is the paradox of serving the one in whose service is perfect freedom[114]! Grasp the duty without the joy and you will end up acting like a driven bully or feeling like a dejected failure. Focus only on the privilege without remembering that you have a responsibility and other things will distract you. For myself, I would always rather lean into the privilege and act out of gratitude, but both are essential for those who accept the invitation to take up their own cross.

Such, then, is the invitation to all saved by the cross: come and join in the mission of God. It will cost you everything, but last for all eternity and without a doubt be the best thing you ever do with your life!

---

[114] The second collect (prayer) in the Church of England's 1662 Book of Common Prayer is

O God, who art the author of peace and lover of concord,
in knowledge of whom standeth our eternal life,
whose service is perfect freedom:
Defend us thy humble servants in all assaults of our enemies;
that we, surely trusting in thy defence,
may not fear the power of any adversaries;
through the might of Jesus Christ our Lord. Amen.

The phrase in question is far older, though, translating an ancient Latin prayer.

5A – PAUSING FOR BREATH

Pause for a moment and consider...

What issues are you wrestling with that have caused you to pick up this book?

If the following questions are useful, please use them to reflect:

1) What have I noticed the Spirit of saying to me in this chapter?
   a) What have I learned?
   b) Where do I want to reflect further?
   c) What ideas will not go away?
2) What are my priorities and how do they line up with Christ's?
3) To whom am I sent and how must I go?
4) What prevents those around me hearing the good news, and is there anything I can do about this?
5) What do I need to do in response to what God is saying to me?

A PAUSING AND A SUMMARY

So, where have we got to in all of this? This is not really a conclusion as the journey is still to continue with the other two themes. This is less of an arrival point, and rather more of a pause at the end of a good day's travel, knowing that there is more to come tomorrow.

I have set out to sort out my head on the question of whether it is possible to inhabit this tension faithfully. Can we find life in the place between opposing challenges, the territory these books call the space between the stones and the firelight? In allowing myself to be recaptured by the cross I have been captivated again by the work of God in reconciling the irreconcilable and commissioning his people to inhabit the vacuum between holiness and daily life: the grace-space which is only possible when held in the heart of God.

I will journey on in the next two books in this series, not least into the territory of the second-covenant exile and the dance of the powerless. You are warmly invited to join me on that journey if you would like to, but let's notice what we have noticed first. I don't pretend that I have addressed the questions everyone seems to be asking about sexuality, but I do find myself equipped just a little better to understand my vocation when it comes to standing between those of apparently irreconcilable views.

In particular there are four things with which I find myself living as I look back on this part of my own journey:

The daily living of the cross

The realisation that my daily life is meant to inhabit, extend, and effect the work of the cross (which we explored in chapter 2) is profoundly releasing for me. I do not need to get everything right the first time I face it. I do not need to know all the answers. I do not need to be certain. I do not need to be infallible. I do need to hold on, to pray, to love, and to stick with it. I need to cling to the cross of Christ and not put my own cross down.

This is my vocation to carry my cross for the extension of the work of Christ among those around me. It is not done for personal piety, reward, clarity, or admiration. I am called into crucified life because this is what it is to follow Christ. This is what it is to join in his mission. This is what the world needs, God requires, and my aching humanity was always created to be able to do. This is the vocation of the returning younger son[115] as he inhabits the work of the father. It is the father's searching, rescuing, reconciling work and it is not done yet.

The deep reality of the cross

Secondly, I am profoundly moved by the profundity of engagement that we see on the cross. Others may not fall into this trap, but I find myself all-too-quickly confining the cross to the religious parts of my life and thus diminishing it almost completely. Lock the cross in the church and it becomes an irrelevance to the world and the greatest travesty in history. Reduce it to jewellery, decoration, iconography, or religious symbolism and there is no covenant of grace.

The cross is the raw, gritty, engaged, utterly real centre of the love of God and it is planted in the deepest heart of our brokenness. There is nothing that is not embraced, engaged,

---

[115] We will return to explore this further in chapter 4 of book 3.

and transformed by the cross. There is nothing that shocks, horrifies, repels, or withstands the crucified Christ, and there is no situation in which we are trapped that is beyond the reach of the cross. It was enabled through humanity's worst and deepest rebellion as God was most ultimately rejected, and in that place it brought victory and freedom.

We never need to make ourselves (or attempt to make others) clean before we come to the cross. This is not a posh dinner or a meeting of the would-be in-laws. This is emergency surgery. It is a child in burning building. It is a hostage longing to be rescued. We leap into the arms of the cross just as we are without any hope or plea but for the cross itself. And in this place we rediscover God's extraordinary graceful power.

The simplicity of the cross

Thirdly, I am delightedly and slightly embarrassed to say, I rediscover the childlike (but never childish) simplicity of the cross. It stands both literally and metaphorically shining a silhouette of life in the simplest of forms over human history, inviting all who will see it to enter. All can see, all can understand (at least, all can understand enough, we will never fully understand the cross), all can receive, and all can find life.

In my own devotional life as I have wrestled with this material, I think that this is the thing I come back to again and again. There are so many things that come over my desk which demand far more wisdom than I could ever have and far more grace than ever seems attainable in this life. But the cross tells a different story. It is not that it makes the complexity itself simple, but it does stand as the simplest, clearest, and most solitary of entry points into the way of life. It would be easy to be ashamed of the simplicity of this good news, but like Paul before us[116] we must not and may not be.

---

[116] See Romans 1.16

The sufficiency of the cross

And this is my final resting place. The cross really does deal with it all. I am often tempted to add to the work of redemption but there is no more that can be or needs to be done. We too often preach repentance as if it were an additional work of salvation (and we shall return to this in the third chapter of the next book). We speak as if it is our task to clean ourselves up before God stamps the deal with the mark of Calvary, but repentance could not be further from this. True repentance is the chosen alignment of our lives with grace one stumbling step at a time, rather than some self-cleansing work of spiritual supererogation. True repentance always relies on God far more than it ever could on me; it points to him, glorifies him, and serves him infinitely more than it highlights me, magnifies me, or furthers my own ends.

One more thought as we, in our own reading and praying, continue to consider major issues that affect us today. I am more and more convinced that 'the issue of the day' in the New Testament was the eating of meat sacrificed to idols. It recurs as a theme in too many places[117], and is too central to the first council of the church for it to be anything other than a major controversy. I am intrigued that the apostle Paul seems to teach in a manner contrary to the decree of the first Jerusalem council on this subject, but what matters in this place and for now is that the cross was big enough to span this divide within the early church. If that was true of that issue in that place, it is true now for all that we face, and will be for all eternity.

> Lord of life
> Held on high on the cross

---

[117] See Acts 15 in which early Christians are instructed to abstain from food sacrificed to idols, and Acts 21 in which this is repeated. Note, too, Romans 14, Romans 15, 1 Corinthians 8, and 1 Corinthians 10 where it is discussed (and allowed)

Enable us afresh to come to you
in the freedom of humility and the joy of trusting,
both in our hopefulness and fear
Finding life and peace
in all we do and are
Through your grace and in your mercy
Amen

Epilogue

You might like to listen to this before reading on
(it was designed to be heard more than read),
but it's up to you.

I can still taste the words, sick though they make me to the very stomach. It's the firelight. It's the warmth. It's the disarming invitation to belong. I am right back there in the violent inner awakening of the moment.

That moment.

Utter darkness in the firelight.

Faithless fool... in the firelight.

I don't fu... *I can't bring myself to say it...* I DON'T know him.

And the voices still surround me... their taunting, stinging tone still stuck like barbs in the flesh of my soul... my conscience.

- But you're Cephas, Rocky, his mate, aren't you?

- Yes, or at least you are just like him... the big, dumb one who followed him everywhere?

- My Lord and my God... oooh I just love it when you call me Cephas... my big, strong, dependable, rock...

I DON'T F-ING KNOW WHAT YOU ARE TALKING ABOUT, YOU PONCY BLOODY SOUTHERN TOFFS... *and out poured all my vitriol... my racism, my sexism, my profanity... a kind of verbal torrent of foul blasphemous stream-of-consciousness vomit. At another time it might almost have been confession, but now it was hurled as a kind of offensive defence...*

... defence against the charge of being his.

His Cephas... on the rocks. Broken against that which was much tougher than I would ever be.

I will never leave you or forsake you. Cephas. Simon.

I don't f-ing know what you are talking about.

And will you stop calling me that name? he gave that to me, and I have never once lived up to it.

Simon, son of John...

Just STOP IT, will you... the fire... it was so appealing, so inviting. It is so appealing, so inviting. A bit of warmth. A touch of kindness. An invitation... but to what? A little human contact for the abandoned rock on the rocks... it's the same, and yet it isn't. There is something more than human contact here.

Simon, son of John...

Simon... It's all I will ever be. Simon, the fisherman's son. It's where I learned it all. The foul language I was shocked to find I still spoke like a native. The instinct to fight. The need to fit in. The deep practical get-it-done approach that was more interested in what worked than what was right. The loyalty... that was what I had lost.

Huh! Fishing for people? I thought I had been caught so securely... but now? But then?

Simon, son of John, do you love me?

That was the question, you see... and the fire... and the smell of cooking food... and the warmth of companionship... and – well, frankly, stuff the rights and wrongs: what I had said I would do. Did I love him? Would I really go to my death for him? As he revealed himself to be?

Do I love him?

Lord, you know I love you... I am so rubbish at sticking to it, rubbish at saying it, rubbish at standing up for it, rubbish even at loving you... but I love you.

Simon, son of John, do you love me more than these?

I still don't know what he means: more than they do? Hardly! And yet yes, YES – with all my heart, YES... but they didn't abandon him, deny him, only to be accused from the mouth of a rooster. More than these things... these fishing things... the familiarity of a trade well known.

Simon, son of John, do you love me?

I do! Lord, you know I do... and I will try to feed, to be faithful, true, a solid pebble even when I struggle to be a rock... but I don't know how, and I don't know with what, and all the solid certainty I thought I had... shattered with the crowing of that flaming cock...

And in the firelight, this firelight, can the place of faithlessness really become the place of restoration... of healing, of grace... the place of not letting go...

Utter grace in the firelight.

Found... refound... profound... abounding grace hounding me relentlessly, kindly... binding, blinding, finding, minding, guiding, inviting, healing me... taking, breaking, shaking, making, waking, beckoning me... in the firelight I will be faithful... one step at a time.

Do you love me?

I do. I will. I know not how, but I'm not letting go, and I do love you...

And on this rock I will build my church.

Appendix: Noting our Setting

As I said in the introduction, my own reflective journey leading to this book has been lengthy. This is not the point of the book, but you will have your own journey and sharing this part of mine might help your own framing of the kind of questions with which we are wrestling.

Here, then, let me offer you three introductions which reflect this: a personal one, a churchy one, and a wider societal one. All are part of my own journey, but none are finished and none define me (only Christ can truly do that). I simply hope that in noting them I can share some awareness of the factors that seem to influence me.

It might be that sexuality is at the forefront of our thoughts (or it might not), but please do allow your mind and heart to range more widely as you search the scriptures and pray. This has been my testimony in exploring this material, and I am grateful.

A personal introduction

If you ask about sexuality in the context of discipleship, I realise I am caught in tensions that pull me in opposing directions, and as I look around I see that I am very far from being alone. It is all too easy to attend to the strident, clarion calls of those who claim to be clear on the issues at hand and allow the heart, soul, even the mind, to be pushed first one way and then another. We who seek to follow Christ with open ears, minds, and hearts can often find that we seem to be called in two or more directions at the same time. In popular debates about human identity, sexuality, and gender the headlines are simple to identify, but the living is really tricky. Even if you take Christian tradition and teaching (indeed pretty much any religious perspective, whatever your understanding) out of the picture this area is not straightforward. We in the church can live with the easy idea that others find this simple, but that is far from true. Look at debates around sports, about who can change in which changing rooms, or about how children are taught in schools and it is plain that we are dealing with vast complexity.

Those of us who wish to be faithful to Christ (and there are a great many of us, probably far more of us than any one of us might see at any one time) are pulled between the way of welcome and love and the way of loyalty to revelation which lies beyond our own culture or understanding. The tension exists whether we read the Bible as it has traditionally been read with regard to relationships but live in a world that thinks differently, or we read the Bible in a manner which embraces diverse understandings of sexual identity but love and value those who struggle with such development of orthodoxy. We are caught between what I have come to think of as the stones and the firelight, and there are few resources to help us stay sane and faithful in the messy middle ground of struggling discipleship, let alone in our own faltering attempts at wise leadership.

I started scribbling the material that has eventually ended up in this form because it felt to me as if my nose was constantly held so close to the wood that I could not see the trees and I wanted space to think, pray, ponder, and worship. It felt like there was more going on, but my head and my heart both felt full to bursting point and I needed space to step back and consider. I felt, indeed I feel, that there is more going on than I easily see and that I need to grapple with it, but I could not find safe space to explore it. Exploration requires the space to be wrong, and it is quite dangerous if bishops try to work stuff out on the hoof. Thus I, too, started with sexuality even though it is not where I would choose to start these reflections. This is where pressing and apparently irreconcilable questions are currently being thrust upon me most forcibly (although it is not the only arena in which this is happening). This is where I began to wonder what God was up to behind the sound and fury of current debates.

I began my scribbling holding my Bible in one hand and five books in the other. I continue grappling with my Bible (ever more urgently, it seems) as the breadth of my pondering increases and the debate gets louder; studying day by day, and doing so with my mind, but also with my heart, soul, and in practice. I do consider (although do not plan to expound that consideration here) that this can be well understood as seeking cognitive understanding, mature emotional engagement, spiritual wisdom, and practical formation of life. Thus, I want to know more about the Bible, but I also want to inhabit it, and let it inhabit me. This is where the reflections (or lectios[118]) that punctuate this series come from; they are not merely intellectual exercises. It is also where the themes of the book come from: 'how can such a sentence be changed by such a sentence', I find myself asking at the end of the first lectio (the reflection on page 1). The answer, of course, is that it can only be changed by the cross, and the woman in that event is powerless (as we all are) in front of God, just as she is in front of her accusers. This reflection draws me deeply into pondering the cross and our own powerlessness, and the huge and much overlooked (at least in the modern Western world) biblical theme of exile that seems to me to bind those two together.

Each of the five modern books I held as I began this series of reflections have been written by people I know personally.

---

[118] The reflections at the beginning and end of the book and which frame each section.

Every one of these authors (four men and one woman, four gay (or 'same-sex-attracted' as one would prefer to define themself although others would find that hard) and one straight) has a clear and influential faith in Christ. I have grown in my own discipleship through knowing them, and I have seen others do the same. I don't agree with everything in all of the books, and the books themselves don't agree with each other, but I know these people and respect them each for different reasons. I value their fellowship and their faith and it grieves me that I am not sure each knows the value I place on them; disagreement is really hard to navigate well. If I look at myself and consider my experience of the church, it seems to me that we quickly pigeon hole each other and make all manner of assumptions about what others believe. We often give the impression of being pretty hopeless when it comes to listening to each other, and we struggle to believe that someone can disagree with us without writing us off.

This has really serious consequences when it comes to sexuality.

There are so many stories of anguish and pain in this area. It is likely that you will either have your own, or know personally those whose experience this is. You will certainly have come across them in the media. Some will seem to have been resolved, many simply go on being deeply painful, and a few end in the worst kind of tragedy (self-harming and even suicide in instances I know of, for example). Sometimes the church is found to be deeply supportive in these situations, at other times (or for other people, sometimes) the experience is not positive, and can be immensely hard. Even having spent considerable time listening, accompanying, and praying with people with a whole range of experience, I know that I cannot begin to plumb the depths of the agonies that someone endures as they wrestle with everything they understood to be their own identity as a human being and the conflict they experience with their faith and their Christian family. I don't need to know someone's situation, agree with it, or share it to be horrified, grieved, and penitent that we can find ourselves in a situation where someone feels that the only way out is self-destructive and harmful.

Read Vicky Beeching's book, Undivided[119], which is one of the tomes sitting by my computer as I write. You don't need to agree with her conclusions or even her arguments to hear what she is saying and be moved by it. Listen with your heart as well as your head and look beyond whatever strongly held views you may have on these issues, and tell me that you do not grieve over the situations she repeatedly found herself in. She is very honest about the harrowing impact of holding her gay identity in the context of active faithful Christian communities.

Equally, we cannot simply respond to such situations by throwing out two millennia of Christian teaching, the (at least apparently) clear teaching of the Bible, or the communion that we share with billions of Christians around the world who hold a traditional understanding of Christian teaching in the area of sexuality and relationship. If you are reading these words without your own experience of following Christ personally (and please know that you are most welcome in this space whatever your own faith might be) these might sound like very strange things to value compared with someone's wellbeing or identity. However, for Christians, our primary identity is in Christ, and our understanding of all things is shaped by what we believe to be God's self-revelation in the Bible. It is far from new to apply this to sexuality: monogamy, celibacy, abstinence, and fidelity are all expressions of Christian sexuality. Have a look at Ed Shaw's 'Plausibility Problem'[120], and you will see an eloquent and lengthy exploration of this traditional and almost universal strand of Christian identity and teaching.

---

[119] Beeching, V - *Undivided: Coming Out, Becoming Whole, and Living Free From Shame* (William Collins, 2019)

[120] Shaw, E - *The Plausibility Problem: The Church And Same-Sex Attraction* (IVP, 2015)

We cannot and must not ignore the Bible, and neither can we pretend that it says something it doesn't. Just the other day someone assured me, quite seriously, that they were convinced Paul was gay because it made sense of so much of what he wrote. David and Jonathan are fairly commonly portrayed as active or repressed gay lovers. Of course it is possible that these assertions are right and that there is more behind one or both of the assertions than I have yet understood. However, when these memes have come up in conversation, I have not been given any compelling or academically rigorous argument that might allow for them to become axiomatic or orthodox interpretations of the biblical text. Never mind, for now, what any of us might wish to be the case; we don't establish a new norm simply by wishing it into being or asserting it as truth, whatever modern culture might suggest in this regard. Christianity that models itself methodologically on the inventiveness of a post-truth society will crumble.

The point is that we, who take our faith seriously and live in the West in the 21st Century, find ourselves in what can appear to be an impossible place; trapped between clear Christian teaching on the one hand and a deep dogmatic belief about human identity in the world around us. I don't think I need to set out the positions; others do so far more clearly than I could, but we do need to face up to the fact that they are not reconcilable by any logic or clever theology. I have seen many such attempts which persuade some faithful Christians one way or another, but none that has managed to persuade all that one side or the other of this argument is right… and that's assuming that there are only two sides to a discussion which is very far from being binary.

It can seem like we face a binary choice between abandoning a biblical faith or abandoning the world, between asserting one incomplete truth or asserting another, and I have to say that I am not content with either. I cannot let go of either, not because (or at least not *just* because) I want my cake and I want to eat it, but because I can't see the Bible allowing me to let go of either. I may neither assert that the Bible or traditional Christian teaching says something it clearly doesn't, nor assert a 'truth' about humanity which lies so far beyond the grasp of a millennial or post-millennial Christian that the only way they can escape it is to take their own life. It seems to me that my vocation as a Christ-following cross-carrier is somehow to stand in exactly this gap between two apparently irreconcilable positions.

This is what I am wrestling with as I write... and I realise I am not alone (either in the sense of being the only one thinking about this, or in the sense of thinking in isolation from others), so let me say two things.

Firstly, I freely confess that I have written more for my own sanity than to guide others. I am deeply committed to trying to listen more than I speak, not least in areas that go deep into another's experience of the gift of life, and this just means that my head gets very full of stuff that it is not always helpful to process out loud or in that moment. Thus I have scribbled things down to process them (and only later realised I ought to share them), but as I do so my imaginary audience are key in testing my thinking and wrestling. Can I be faithful, compassionate, and missional in holding all this together? I am trying to engage with the Scriptures, with the wellbeing of others, with my experience of seeking to live faithfully, with the traditions within which we are located, and with the missiological impact of having this debate in public. The thoughts are too big for the inside of my head!

Moreover, though, as I wrestle with the question of how I remain faithful, sane, and grounded in the world in which I am rooted and to which I am sent, I note how often I hear in others the same tension I find in myself: how do we stay faithful to the faith we have inherited, true to our Lord and King, both in doctrinal truth and in following the ways of love and grace he embodied and taught? When another person believes with all their heart that their very identity is inextricably linked with an aspect of humanity which seems to me contrary to the faith I have received, but sees no contradiction in such an assertion, how, together, do we discharge our God-given duties of loving service, true fellowship, and faithful witness? How, in other words, do we walk the way of Peter in struggling to remain faithful whatever the cost, and the unnamed witness in dropping our stones. How do we live between the stones and the firelight? This is not just a matter for private pondering: although I am also deeply aware that the public version of this material is a poor, humble, and incomplete gift of some potential resources for others who struggle in this place. It is far from complete, but it is a start.

Secondly, I find I am less and less convinced that we are asking the right questions or focussing on the right issues. We know the terrain around our own navels on these questions very well, and simply cannot find a way to bridge the difference between 'innies' and 'outies' by arguing. We are like a lorry that finds itself stuck in increasingly narrow roads and unable either to get through or to turn around, or like an addict who knows that there are no real answers in habitual behaviour, but cannot find any other form of answer. The damage that we are doing to ourselves, each other, and the mission of God is palpable, and we need to find ways to engage in a whole new order of conversation... for the sake of the lost and desperate if nothing else.

And this is why I am exploring this thinking in this way, in conversation with imagined interlocutors before whom I set out my case and cross-examine my own thinking. It is why I am doing more than making notes as I sort out my head; indeed what I have just described as 'my case' is not actually a case at all yet, I need to let it emerge to see what it is as I refuse to look away either from the world around me or the text in front of me. I don't want a party-line to defend, but I am sorry to say that I have yet to find a context in which I can explore this with others without having to deal with the various party lines that are engraved both in me and in others. We must wrestle with the Scriptures even when they leave us limping, but also remember that wrestling that doesn't change, and even wound, us probably isn't really wrestling. It is why attentive, compassionate listening matters, and why the search for wisdom and grace in this complex and contended area of our shared life is so vital. It might seem like the question before us is sexuality, but there are much bigger issues to be addressed which draw us into the question of how we engage with massive difference in the church. Might it be that recognising, and maybe even asking, the bigger questions begins to open up a viable way of approaching such issues which makes space for those who are seeking Christ but do not know if they can trust those who follow him?

A (Western) cultural introduction

There is another introductory thought that I want to offer you, although I do so tentatively knowing myself not to be an expert sociologist. However, one of the reasons that I think this material matters when it comes to thinking about sexuality (and that it will matter when it comes to thinking about other difficult questions) is that those around us make decisions in a manner very different to the ones that are encouraged by faith. The wider world will often simply not spot why things matter (or even what matters) to us as Christians, for without God as the anchor-point of reflection, processing, action, and understanding, people see stuff through very different eyes. Without Christ they start in a very different place when it comes to understanding a person's own identity. We, as Christians, are blind if we think that this conglomeration of views and approaches (it is far from uniform) does not affect us, for we live in a particular time and place and get carried along, shaped, and influenced just as much as the next person. In the daily round, we can be very naïve about the dominance of shared culture. It shapes us, it shapes our children, our friends, our fellow believers, our media, and our world. There are both good and bad things here, and worrying stuff too, but this is not my point: we need to notice and to try not to be surprised by its power. Thus, I am not setting out to argue against things we see in the world about us, simply to look and try to understand in order that we might love effectively and communicate clearly.

Today, if I may succumb to the temptation of broad generalisation for a moment, we have not so much made up our mind on questions of identity and their link to sexuality and gender, we have made up our heart. The 'hive mind' feels very clear on these issues, and this is not a question of an embodied philosophical construct, so much as a coalition of feelings which appear to cohere around acceptance, to such an extent that they don't need to be consistent, identical, or even logical. This might frustrate those who want to critique the positions others hold, but it does not actually invalidate the thinking... or the feeling. I notice that the popular mind around inclusion is almost a kind of faith position in that it is deeply held and neither needs to rest on consistent foundations nor be taken to its extremes.

We act and talk as if answers to such questions are a matter of self-evident truth and hold them as a matter of dogma and principle. We needn't define our own thinking precisely, but we may condemn those who disagree with us. We speak as if we have some logical philosophy by which we have become convinced, but do so in a manner which negates the need to question. Consequently, whilst there are indubitably some fundamental axioms guiding our thoughts and feelings, they do not need to be consistent, and they do not need to bear the weight of cold rational analysis.

This came home to me when I heard Nigel Owens, the superb Rugby Union referee, on Radio 4's Today programme saying "*I can choose my religion, but I cannot choose my sexuality[121]*". This statement is in marked contrast with most religious

---

[121] BBC Radio 4, Today Programme, 18th May 2019

understanding down the ages, at the very least when it comes to the first half of his sentence, particularly for Judaism, Christianity, and Islam. His intent did not seem to be particularly proselytic, though, he was simply stating facts as he sees them. For him: religion is a matter of consumer choice, sexuality is a given fact.

To some Christian ears statements like this can sound like a campaign to change our beliefs, but I am not sure they are; they are simply a statement of perceived fact. The logic is clear and leads to obvious questions like: why would we not accept someone just as they are? A woman who identifies as a man harms no-one and can only be fully part of society if they discover who they really are, inhabit that identity, and are then able to be comfortable in their own skin. How is it anything but cruel to oppose this? Whoever we are and whatever our views, if we are to consider who we are today, we need to step back and notice the breakdown in communication and understanding with which we are surrounded. We may never fully understand or agree with each other, but it is always good to listen, notice, and care.

These, and other, stories are part of our daily life. They do not define us, but they do affect us and this is a good thing: following Jesus takes place in the real world of everyday life. This is where we pray, where we worship, where we grow, where we reach out in mission, and where we find grace. Attending to the stories of those around us and doing so openly and honestly is part of growing in that faith.

An ecclesiological (churchy) introduction

Finally, in this snapshot, let me note something about our church context (or, actually, let me quote Archbishop Justin as he says it better). For those reading from outside the Diocese of Chester, let me say that I have already let slip that I am a bishop, and to save you having to type me into an internet search engine let me just explain that I am a bishop in the Church of England. We are part of the Anglican Communion, a global fellowship of 80 million Christians across 45 member churches, covering most of the nations of the world.

In 2022, 650 bishops gathered for the Lambeth Conference, and if you listened to the popular press you might have thought that all we talked about was sexuality. In reality it was an extraordinary time of worship, fellowship, and missional focus around issues of justice, evangelism, science, climate change, and human dignity. However, we also looked four-square into the truth that we do not agree when it comes to our understanding of sexuality despite our faithfulness to Christ. We did not fall out, but we did share the reality of the pain and the hope that we feel.

Archbishop Justin addressed the conference at the start of the session in which this was discussed, saying:

> This is one of the most important sessions of this Conference. In it, we come to a question – of what we believe about human dignity, including sexuality – that is deeply dividing, not only for Anglicans but for every part of God's global church.

> This conference is one of the few places that we can meet and be honest with each other about what we think, listen to others and pray together. In some churches, like the Anglican Communion, the disagreement is open. In others it is behind locked doors. But in all it is real. And in all the subject is of the greatest importance.

> Most of the Call on Human Dignity (including sexuality) is uncontentious. None of us would want to argue for sexual violence in conflict, abuse of the vulnerable or violence against minorities or women.

> But paragraph 2.3 is very different. For some here it will be a great relief. There is no attempt being made to alter the historic teaching of the vast majority of Churches of the Anglican Communion. For some, this paragraph will be hugely painful, agonizing emotionally, for it is felt by many to state

that who they are and who they love is wrong, that they are less than fully human.

So in this very brief address, please let me state some important principles.

First, the Call is about Human Dignity and also about Sexuality. The reason the two are combined is that its central theological foundation is that all human beings are of equal worth, loved by God and are those for whom Jesus died on the Cross and rose to life. As St Paul says again and again in Romans "there is no distinction".

Second, as we discuss this, we are all vulnerable.

For the large majority of the Anglican Communion the traditional understanding of marriage is something that is understood, accepted and without question, not only by Bishops but their entire Church, and the societies in which they live. For them, to question this teaching is unthinkable, and in many countries would make the church a victim of derision, contempt and even attack. For many churches to change traditional teaching challenges their very existence.

For a minority, we can say almost the same. They have not arrived lightly at their ideas that traditional teaching needs to change. They are not careless about scripture. They do not reject Christ. But they have come to a different view on sexuality after long prayer, deep study and reflection on understandings of human nature. For them, to question this different teaching is unthinkable, and in many countries is making the church a victim of derision, contempt and even attack. For these churches not to change traditional teaching challenges their very existence.

So let us not treat each other lightly or carelessly. We are deeply divided. That will not end soon. We are called by Christ himself both to truth and unity.

Third, there is no attempt to change people's minds in this Call. It states as a fact that the vast majority of Anglicans in the large majority of Provinces and Dioceses do not believe that a change in teaching is right. Therefore, it is the case that the whole of Lambeth 1.10 1998 still exists. This Call does not in any way question the validity of that resolution. The Call states that many Provinces – and I say again, I think we need to acknowledge it's the majority – continue to affirm that same-gender marriage is not permissible. The Call also states that other provinces have blessed and welcomed same sex union or marriage, after careful theological reflection and a process of reception.

In that way, it states the reality of life in the Communion today. As is said in the letter, and I re-emphasise, there is no mention of sanctions, or exclusion, in 1.10 1998. There is much mention of pastoral care. As Lambeth 1.10 also states: "all baptised, believing and faithful persons, regardless of sexual orientation are full members of the Body of Christ" and to be welcomed, cared for, and treated with respect (I.10, 1998).

Fourth, many people are watching and listening, both inside and outside the Church. But we Bishops, you alone and I are responsible for what is decided on this Call. When we will all answer to God on the day of judgement, we will not be able to say – and there is no vote today, but when at some point if ever we make a decision on this – we will not be able to say that I voted this or that way because others told me to. Please therefore be present, in this room or online, today. Do not spend the time looking on your phone at what others outside the room are saying. You are the shepherds of your flock as I am the shepherd of the flock that I serve. Let us not act in a way that disgraces our witness. Speak frankly, but in love.

Finally, a short comment on my own thinking. I am very conscious that the Archbishop of Canterbury is to be a focus of unity and is an Instrument of Communion. That is a priority. Truth and unity must be held together, but Church history also says that this sometimes takes a very long time to reach a point where different teaching is rejected or received. I neither have, nor do I seek, the authority to discipline or exclude a church of the Anglican Communion. I will not do so. I may comment in public on occasions, but that is all. We are a Communion of Churches, not a single church.

I want to end by repeating this line from the Call on Human Dignity: "As Bishops we remain committed to listening and walking together to the maximum possible degree, despite our deep disagreement on these issues."

Sisters and brothers, may I thank you for your patience in listening to me.[122]

I reproduce this verbatim as it captures exactly the tension we are exploring, and gives rise to the question we have set out to explore in the main body of the text.

All of these factors influence our thinking, our feeling, our reading of the bible, and our relating. I note them to help me (and possibly you) notice them. My prayer, though, is that the material of this book will draw you back to the Scriptures themselves, to the Lord, and to the pursuit of holiness and faith in your daily life. The Lord is very far from finished with his works of grace.

---

[122] Full text available via little-house-in-joppa.uk/S&F202332

BIBLE REFERENCES

Wild and Majestic

Romantic Visions of Scotland

Patrick Watt and Rosie Waine

National
Museums
Scotland

Wild and majestic
Romantic Visions of Scotland

Exhibition at
National Museum of Scotland
Chambers Street
Edinburgh EH1 1JF

www.nms.ac.uk

26 June to 10 November 2019

Exhibition kindly sponsored by
Baillie Gifford Investment Managers

Book published in 2019 by
NMS Enterprises Limited – Publishing
a division of NMS Enterprises Limited
National Museums Scotland
Chambers Street
Edinburgh EH1 1JF

www.nms.ac.uk

**British Library Cataloguing in Publication
Data**
A catalogue record of this book is available
from the British Library.

ISBN 978 1 910682 24 1

Typesetting by NMS Enterprises Limited –
Publishing.
Cover and design by Mark Blackadder
based on exhibition design by NMS
Exhibitions and Design.

Photography (unless otherwise credited) by
NMS Photography.
Printed and bound in Great Britain by
Claro Print, Glasgow.
Cover: (front) *Colonel William Gordon of
Fyvie*, by Pompeo Batoni (1708–87),
1766, National Trust for Scotland,
Fyvie Castle; (back) © Lochnagar, HES
(Aerofilm Collection).
Page 1: Plaid brooch, said to have been
presented to John Ban MacKenzie by
Queen Victoria, *c*.1854, National
Museums Scotland.

'Gaelic Voices' text

By Dr Domhnall Uilleam Stiùbhart and
Professor Hugh Cheape, Sabhal Mòr
Ostaig, University of the Highlands and
Islands, in partnership with National
Museums Scotland, on the production of
content for the exhibition *Wild and
Majestic: Romantic Visions of Scotland*.

For a full listing of NMS Enterprises Limited
– Publishing titles, and related merchandise,
go to:

www.nms.ac.uk/books

Contents

Oh! for the crags that are wild and majestic,
The steep, frowning glories of dark Loch na garr.

George Gordon, Lord Byron, *Lachin Y. Gair*, 1807

Wild and majestic

Romantic visions of Scotland

For the poet Lord Byron the mountainous landscapes of the Grampian Highlands inspired an emotional response, one that characterised Scotland as a land of wilderness, heroism and history. Byron was one of many writers, musicians and artists of the Romantic movement whose work reflected growing international fascination with the distinctive culture of the Scottish Highlands and Islands. By the end of the 19th century, a romantic vision of Gaelic society and history had come to stand for all of Scotland in the popular imagination.

This picture of Scotland's past has always been controversial and some people have suggested it is a distortion of history. This exhibition traces the origins of that vision and explores how the relationship between romance and reality has created an image of Scotland which still endures today.

Left: George Gordon, Lord Byron

In 1796, aged eight, Byron was taken by his mother from their home in Aberdeen to the Highlands to recover from a bout of scarlet fever. He was captivated by the atmosphere of Lochnagar, an imposing mountain which overlooks the River Dee. Eleven years later, Byron recalled the mountain and used it as the romantic inspiration for 'Lachin Y. Gair', which appeared in *Hours of Idleness*, his first collection of poems, published in 1807.

By Henry Pierce Bone (1779–1855), early 19th century, National Museums Scotland

Background: *A View of Lochnagar*

The mountain of Lochnagar rises above the Balmoral estate in the Grampian Highlands. Queen Victoria gave this painting to Prince Albert as a Christmas present in 1848.

By James Giles (1801–70), 1848, oil on panel, Royal Collection Trust / © Her Majesty Queen Elizabeth II 2019

Symbols of Scotland

This distinctive style of sword was an essential part of the military culture of 18th-century clan society. In the perceptions of outsiders, Highlanders could be both idealised as noble warriors or reviled as barbarians and dangerous rebels.

The inscriptions on the blade – 'God save King James the 8' and 'Prosperity to Schotland and no Union' – proclaim the owner's loyalty to the Jacobite cause, for which many Highland clans rose to fight against the established government. Within a generation after it was made, basket-hilted swords like this were carried by Highlanders proudly serving in the British army. With their distinctive uniforms, music and weapons, Highland soldiers became popular symbols of Scotland.

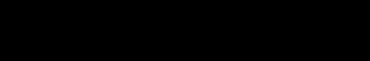

Highland basket-hilted sword

Early to mid-18th century,
National Museums Scotland

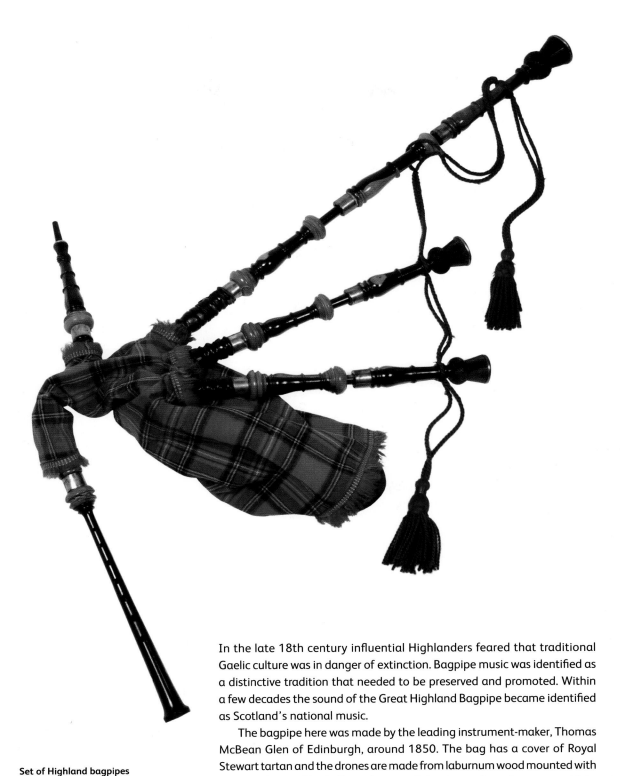

Set of Highland bagpipes

By Thomas McBean Glen (1804–73),
c.1850, National Museums Scotland

In the late 18th century influential Highlanders feared that traditional Gaelic culture was in danger of extinction. Bagpipe music was identified as a distinctive tradition that needed to be preserved and promoted. Within a few decades the sound of the Great Highland Bagpipe became identified as Scotland's national music.

The bagpipe here was made by the leading instrument-maker, Thomas McBean Glen of Edinburgh, around 1850. The bag has a cover of Royal Stewart tartan and the drones are made from laburnum wood mounted with silver and ivory. The bells at the top of the drones have been carved into representations of thistles, Scotland's national flower.

7

The dramatic landscape of the Highlands and Islands is one of the most enduring symbols of Scotland. The picturesque beauty of mountains, lochs and waterfalls inspired generations of artists, musicians and writers.

This painting captures the sublime beauty of Loch Katrine – the setting for Sir Walter Scott's poem 'The Lady of the Lake', which inspired many tourists to visit the loch to experience the romantic landscape for themselves. In the foreground, on the left, tourists are entertained by a tartan-clad piper, while they wait to board a ferry to Ellen's Isle, named after the heroine of Scott's poem.

Background: *Landscape with Tourists at Loch Katrine* [detail]

By John Knox (1778–1845), oil on canvas, National Galleries of Scotland

9

10

The uniform opposite includes all the elements of Highland dress that had become standard by the turn of the 20th century. Due to a combination of fashion, royal patronage and an enduring popular fascination with the past, this style of Highland dress emerged as a form of national costume for Scotland.

The Balmoral Highlanders were established on the royal estate at Balmoral in 1887, during the reign of Queen Victoria. They were formed of 24 men-at-arms and one piper. They acted as the ceremonial clan retinue for the monarch when in residence at Balmoral, adopting the Royal Stewart tartan and the royal crest as part of their uniform.

Opposite: Uniform of the Balmoral Highlanders

*c.*1903, National Museums Scotland

Left: Archibald F Macdonald, Jäger to His Royal Highness the Prince of Wales

This portrait is one of a series of sketches of Balmoral retainers, by Kenneth MacLeay, which were commissioned by Queen Victoria. MacLeay worked from life and photographs to create the finished portraits, which, though idealised, are remarkably detailed.

From Kenneth MacLeay, *Highlanders of Scotland: Portraits illustrative of the Principal Clans and Followings, and their Retainers, of the Royal Household at Balmoral, in the reign of Her Majesty Queen Victoria, c.*1870, National Museums Scotland

The Champion and Piper to the Laird of Grant

This pair of portraits depict two important members of the household of the Chief of Clan Grant. They are impressively dressed in Highland clothing tailored in a uniform tartan, and carry the bagpipes and weapons that represent their ceremonial positions in clan society. The portraits were designed to impress visitors to Castle Grant with a sense of the Laird of Grant's traditional authority as a Highland chieftain.

These are not romantic portraits based on an imagined past. The Scottish artist Richard Waitt carefully documented the appearance of these real people. They were painted in 1714, at a time when clan society was being eroded by economic and political pressures, and record a way of life that was already passing into history.

Left: *Champion to the Laird of Grant, Alastair Grant Mor*

The Champion was the strongest fighter in the Laird's retinue. Alastair Grant Mor (Big Alastair Grant) is portrayed brandishing a curved sword known as a turcael and holding his targe, ready to fight for his chief and clan. He was more usually employed in the Laird's timber business.

By Richard Waitt (1708–32), 1714, oil on canvas, © Reidhaven Trust (courtesy of Grantown Museum)

Opposite: *Piper to the Laird of Grant, William Cumming*

William Cumming belonged to a family of trained musicians who served the Lairds of Grant through many generations. Cumming flies the heraldic banner of the Grant family from the drones of his bagpipe. Castle Grant is in the background.

By Richard Waitt (1708–32), 1714, oil on canvas, National Museums Scotland

Scotland after Culloden

The Jacobite rising of 1745 divided loyalties across Britain. Supporters of the exiled House of Stuart were pitted against those who remained loyal to the ruling House of Hanover. Scotland became a battleground. In April 1746, the Jacobite army led by Prince Charles Edward Stuart – 'Bonnie Prince Charlie' – was defeated at the Battle of Culloden.

Violent reprisals followed. In the aftermath of the conflict, the British government targeted the features of traditional Gaelic society which had defined the Jacobite army, including clan regiments, tartan clothing and Highland weaponry. New military garrisons were stationed across the Highlands and Islands, bringing the region under closer government control. These actions accelerated social and economic changes which had already begun to transform the Highland way of life.

Background: *A sketch of the field at the Battle of Culloden*

This watercolour may have been commissioned by the Duke of Cumberland, the victorious commander at the Battle of Culloden. It was drawn by Thomas Sandby who served as Cumberland's draughtsman and private secretary during the last Jacobite rising.

By Thomas Sandby (1721–98), 1746, pen and ink with watercolour over pencil, Royal Collection Trust / © Her Majesty Queen Elizabeth II 2019

Crime and punishment

The British government viewed the clan structure of Gaelic society as a threat. Although some Highland clans had opposed the Jacobites, clan society as a whole was held responsible and punished for rebellion.

Legislation was passed declaring Jacobite leaders outlaws and traitors. Clan chiefs lost their powers of justice. The estates of prominent Jacobites were confiscated. The carrying of weapons was outlawed, bringing Scotland into line with wider European trends.

Highland dress was seen by the government as part of a warrior culture that had to be broken. From 1748, new laws decreed that men and boys could not wear tartan plaids, kilts or trews unless they were serving in the British army. The legislation was interpreted differently across the country, and its effectiveness depended on enforcement by loyal Highland elites.

Below: Fowling gun owned by the Macdonalds of Clanranald

This gun bears the arms of Macdonald of Clanranald. It was possibly presented to a younger son of the chief of Clanranald before he left France to take part in the Jacobite rising of 1745.

Mid-18th century, National Museums Scotland

Opposite: Tartan coat, trimmed with velvet and decorated with Jacobite rose buttons [detail]

Tartan outfits such as this were considered clear symbols of support for the Jacobite cause. This suit was brought home by Augustine Earle of Heydon Hall in Norfolk, who served as a commissioner of excise in Scotland in 1746, possibly as a souvenir of the Jacobite defeat.

Mid-18th century. On loan from a Private Collection. Image © National Museums Scotland

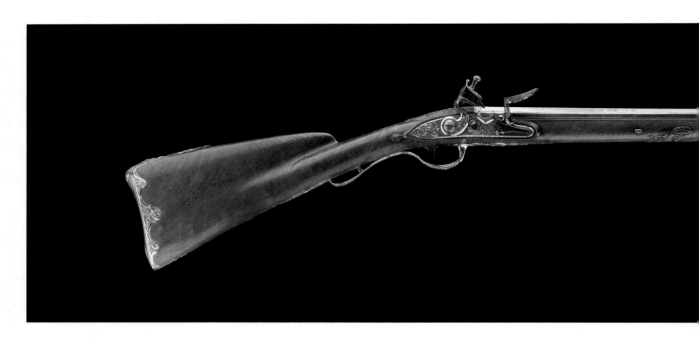

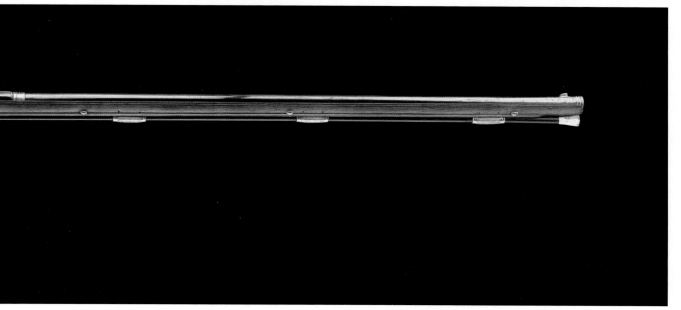

Gaelic voices

The heroes

Since we pulled on the trousers,
We despise that garment,
Tightening about the thighs,
It's a torment to wear;
Before, we were confident
In our belted tartan,
But now our usual clothing
Is rags fit for a pack-horse.

Duncan Bàn Macintyre, *A Song to the Trousers*

After the Battle of Culloden, the outlawing of the tartan plaid, a garment of aristocratic spectacle and display, and its replacement by drab Lowland trousers, was a humiliation widely condemned in Gaelic song. In the trauma that followed the Jacobite defeat, Gaelic bards re-imagined the Jacobite rising of 1745 as a romantic, noble, but doomed enterprise – a consolation in defeat.

Although suspicious tenants often proved reluctant recruits, the chiefs' raising of tartan-clad Highland regiments brought Gaels onto a global stage. Widely-celebrated in Gaelic song, their military heroes and victories reconciled Gaels to the British state. Those veterans who returned home became influential figures in their communities, because of their annual pension, and their store of old soldiers' stories.

Guthan nan Gàidheal

Na curaidhean

Is on a chuir sinn suas am briogais,
Gur neo-measail leinn a' chulaidh ud,
Gan teannadh mu na h-iosgannan,
Gur trioblaideach leinn umainn iad;
'S bha sinn roimhe misneachail,
'S na breacain fo na criosan oirnn,
Ged tha sinn am bitheantas,
A-nise 'cur nan sumag oirnn …

Donnchadh Bàn Mac an t-Saoir, *Òran don Bhriogais*

Às dèidh Chùil Lodair, chaidh èideadh uasal uallach breacan an fhèilidh a thoirmeasg. Dh'fheumadh fireannaich briogaisean odhar Gallda a chur orra: culaidh-nàire bu chuspair do ghrunnan òran Gàidhlig. Anns na bliadhnaichean èiginneach ud, thòisich bàird a' gabhail beachd às ùr mu Bhliadhna Theàrlaich, mar iomairt a bha uasal romansach, ach cuideachd bras, neo-ghlic. Thug seo beagan sòlais dhan fheadhainn a chaill.

Mar bu trice, cha robh mòran aig an t-sluagh mu ghnothaichean saighdearachd, ach thug rèisimeidean nan cinnidhean na Gàidheil, agus am breacan, gu aire an t-saoghail mhòir. Rinn na bàird àrd-mholadh air na gaisgich Ghàidhealach agus na blàran a bhuannaich iad, agus mean air mhean thàinig na Gàidheil gu rèite le rìoghachd Bhreatainn. Na curaidhean a thill le peinnsean bliadhnail agus stòras sgeulachdan mun cuid euchdan, fhuair iad urram mòr sa choimhearsnachd.

The Highland garb is a dress fit only for war, theft and idleness ...

Comment on a draft of the Disarming Act, 1746

20

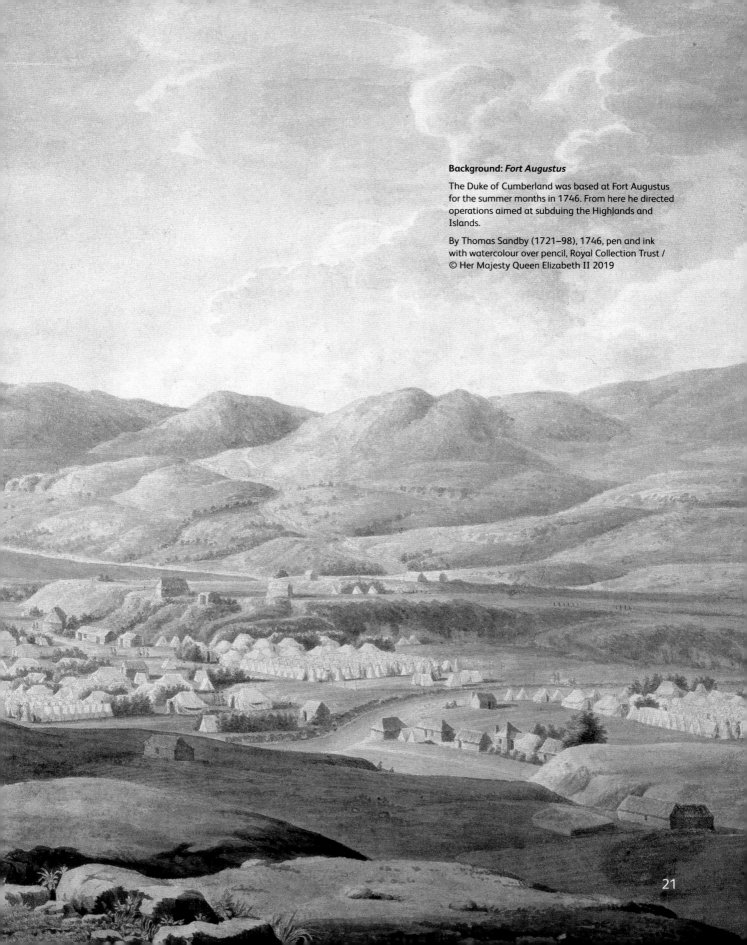

Background: *Fort Augustus*

The Duke of Cumberland was based at Fort Augustus for the summer months in 1746. From here he directed operations aimed at subduing the Highlands and Islands.

By Thomas Sandby (1721–98), 1746, pen and ink with watercolour over pencil, Royal Collection Trust / © Her Majesty Queen Elizabeth II 2019

Sir James Macdonald (1741–66) and Sir Alexander Macdonald (1744/45–95) [detail]

These two boys are the sons of Sir Alexander Macdonald of Sleat, a Highland chieftain with extensive estates on the Isle of Skye. The Macdonalds of Sleat had supported the Jacobites in 1715, but in 1745 they raised a militia in support of the government. Despite the restrictions on wearing Highland dress the boys are shown in tartan outfits, depicting the selective nature of the enforcement of the law.

By William Mosman (1700–71), c.1749, oil on canvas, Scottish National Portrait Gallery

Tartan wedding dress and plaid

This tartan gown and plaid were worn by Isobel (known as Isabella) MacTavish at her wedding to Malcolm Fraser in 1785. The couple lived in Ruthven, near Inverness.

The outfit is a rare surviving example of a tartan costume known to have been worn by a Highland woman during the later 18th century. The gown and plaid are both made of the same tartan, woven from yarns dyed with imported natural dyestuffs such as cochineal and indigo. The gown is lined with homespun linen, probably sourced from the local area.

*c.*1775–85, © Inverness Museum & Art Gallery. Photograph by Ewen Weatherspoon

Natural warriors

After the Battle of Culloden, the British government maintained its military presence in the Highlands and Islands. New fortifications and barracks were built and linked to others constructed in the wake of earlier Jacobite risings. Engineers extended the network of military roads, and military surveyors created the first detailed maps of the Highland terrain.

By 1756, Britain was at war with France and fighting for control of North America. Previously regarded as dangerous rebels, Highlanders were now categorised as natural warriors who could be a source of military manpower for Britain's overseas wars. Highland regiments became part of the British army, bringing the military traditions of clan society into the service of the state.

Highland landowners raised recruits from their estates using their networks of kinship across the region. For landowners, recruiting offered an increase in power, status and revenue. For recruits, military service offered opportunities for financial reward and steady employment.

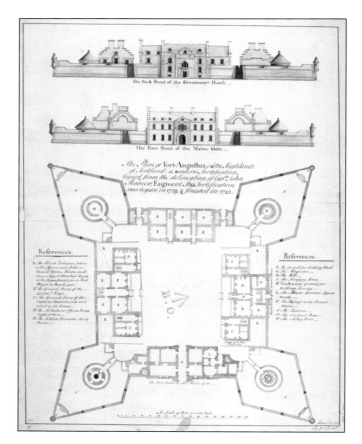

'Sawney in the boghouse'

Satirical prints published in London say much about how Scots could be perceived in late 18th-century Britain. Depictions of all Scots as Highlanders, and of all Highlanders as poor, dirty and cunning, were commonplace. These negative stereotypes endured into the early years of the 19th century.

One popular representation was the character 'Sawney', who became a recognised caricature in anti-Scottish propaganda. Often depicted in crude situations, Sawney perpetuated the idea that Scotland was uncivilised.

This stereotype can be seen as a reaction against the growing influence of Scots in the government and economy of Britain and its Empire. Other popular targets for ridicule during this period included the Irish and French, as well as politicians and the British royal family.

Punch bowl

This punch bowl is decorated with a satirical cartoon known as 'Sawney's Mistake', showing a Highlander in an unfortunate predicament when faced with an unfamiliar latrine. This caricature was first published as a print in 1745, but the image was still popular forty years later.

*c.*1783–85, National Museums Scotland

A romantic vision of Scotland

Across 18th-century Europe, ideas about landscape and history were changing, influenced by the growing Romantic movement in art, literature and music. At a time of rapid economic and political change, the upper and middle classes looked to an idealised past for reassurance, inspiration and excitement.

Parts of the world once thought of as sterile and threatening began to be celebrated as fascinating and dramatic. Scotland, with its mountainous, picturesque landscapes, and its turbulent history, fitted perfectly into this new way of thinking.

The distinctive language, culture and dress of Highland Scots were already thought of as exotic and unspoilt by the modern world. The tragic but heroic story of the lost Jacobite cause had excited an international audience.

In Scotland, growing appreciation of the warrior tradition in Gaelic culture meant that Highlanders were increasingly represented in art and literature as heroic and romantic, rather than as primitive and dangerous.

Opposite: *Colonel William Gordon of Fyvie*

William Gordon was an officer in the 105th Highlanders and nephew to the powerful Duke of Gordon. When his regiment was disbanded in 1763, Gordon embarked on a 'Grand Tour', visiting some of the great European cities. In Rome, he was painted by the artist Pompeo Batoni.

Batoni depicts Gordon in his military uniform; however, his non-regulation plaid, a version of the Huntly tartan, has been arranged to resemble a Roman toga. This portrait represents an early European Romantic view of the Scottish Highlander as a heroic figure, set against a background of classical Roman imagery.

By Pompeo Batoni (1708–87), 1766, oil on canvas, National Trust for Scotland, Fyvie Castle

The Dream of Ossian [detail]

James Macpherson's Ossian poems influenced the wider movement of European Romanticism. This drawing is based on a painting by Jean-Auguste-Dominique Ingres, commissioned by the French Emperor Napoleon Bonaparte in 1811. Napoleon was an Ossian enthusiast and is known to have carried a copy with him on his campaign in Egypt in 1798.

By Jean-Auguste-Dominique Ingres (1780–1867), 1811, Scottish National Gallery of Modern Art

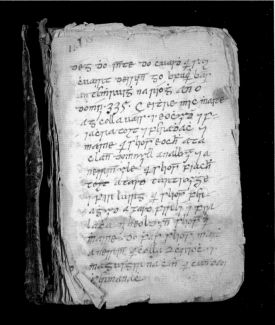

The Ossian sensation

Beginning in 1760, the publication of fragments of the epic poetry of Ossian, a legendary 3rd-century Gaelic bard, introduced the culture of the Scottish Highlands to the world. The Highland schoolmaster and poet, James Macpherson, claimed to have researched and collected ancient tales in the Gaelic language, including work by Ossian, and translated them into English.

Macpherson's Ossian poetry took the literary world by storm. The books were translated into multiple languages and much admired by many influential European writers, artists and composers.

In the midst of Macpherson's success, doubts were raised about the authenticity of his work. Critics suggested that the poetry was a fraud and that Macpherson had written it himself. However, the controversy had little impact on an enthusiastic international audience, fascinated by the idea of a heroic Gaelic past.

Left: Portrait of the writer James Macpherson (1736–96), holding a volume of his Ossian poetry

Ossian was a legendary blind Gaelic bard from the 3rd century and the purported author and narrator of some of the poems collected by Macpherson. Ossian's hero was his father Fingal, King of Morven, in what is now south-west Scotland.

By David Martin (1737–97), late 18th century, oil on canvas. Private Collection, Edinburgh

Right: The Red Book of Clanranald

Macpherson consulted and collected original Gaelic manuscripts belonging to numerous Highland families. These included the Red Book of Clanranald, a volume containing the history and lore of Clan Donald, compiled by a member of the MacMhuirich family of bards.

Late 17th to early 18th century, National Museums Scotland

Gaelic voices

In the age of Ossian

Among the poets who were famous of old in the Scottish Highlands, Ossian was by far the most celebrated. The poems he made were perfect in every virtue with which eloquence could wake the spirit to high thoughts and mighty deeds.

Dùn Èideann, *The Poems of Ossian son of Finn*, 1807

Highlanders recognised that James Macpherson's Ossianic epics drew upon medieval heroic ballads still recited in their communities – albeit blended with tragic, passionate themes borrowed from contemporary love songs.

Enthused by Macpherson's portrayal of an ancient, heroic, emotionally sophisticated Gaelic civilisation, a network of university-educated ministers collected Highland poetry and music, and compiled a Gaelic dictionary, hoping to revitalise their culture. One significant publication was the supposedly genuine Gaelic Ossian – in reality, a slipshod translation of Macpherson's English original.

Guthan nan Gàidheal

Ri linn Oisein

Am measg nam bàrd a bha ainmeil o shean ann an Gàidhealtachd Alba b' e Oisean gu mòr a b' àirde cliù. Bha na duain a rinn e coilionta anns gach buaidh, leis an urrainn teangaireachd an t-anam a mhosgladh gu h-àrd-smaointean agus gu mòr-ghnìomharan.

Dùn Èideann, ***Dàna Oisein mhic Fhinn,*** **1807**

'S math a dh'aithnich Gàidheil gun robh bloighean de sheann laoidhean na Fèinne, laoidhean a chluinnteadh fhathast anns na taighean-cèilidh, ann am mòr-dhàintean Oiseanach Sheumais Bhàin MhicMhuirich. Ach bha cuideachd bròn agus briseadh-cridhe ann a thàinig bho òrain-ghaoil mhuladach a latha fhèin.

Dhealbhaich sgeulachdan MhicMhuirich saoghal àrsaidh Gàidhlig a bha gaisgeil, àilleasach, sìobhalta. Chaidh grunnan mhinistearan Gàidhealach a bheò-ghlacadh leis an dealbh seo. Gus an dualchas aca ath-bheothachadh, rinn iad cruinneachaidhean de sheann cheòl agus bàrdachd, cho math ri briathrachas airson faclair ùr.

Fiù 's nach do nochd deasachadh de dh'Oisean sa Ghàidhlig: na rannan fìrinneach fhèin, mas fhìor. Ann an da-rìribh, ge-tà, cha robh annta ach eadar-theangachadh robach den Bheurla aig MacMhuirich.

A Highland Spirit

Inspired by the Romantic movement, Highland aristocrats, gentlemen and military officers formed clubs and societies dedicated to preserving Gaelic culture and a range of charitable activities.

The Highland Society of London was the first to be formed in 1778. This group of elite Highlanders resident in London took the promotion of their homeland directly to the heart of the British political and cultural establishment. The society campaigned for the restoration of Highland dress, promoted Gaelic language, literature and music, and actively supported Scottish regiments.

Below: *A Highland Dance*

This image of a gathering in the Scottish Highlands shows tartan-clad figures engaged in romanticised Highland pastimes. The men drink whisky and take snuff, while couples dance to the music of the Great Highland Bagpipe.

By David Allan (1744–96), *c.*1780, brush and watercolour over pencil on paper, National Galleries of Scotland. Purchased by the Patrons of the National Galleries of Scotland 1990

Other societies founded during this period championed similar aims. In Edinburgh, the Highland Society of Scotland worked to preserve Gaelic culture and to promote economic development in the Highlands and Islands by encouraging changes in land use. They awarded prizes for essays and inventions that endorsed agricultural reform in the region. Many of the schemes they supported had long lasting implications for the Highland way of life. These clubs also performed a social function, allowing Highlanders to gather together and celebrate what they described as a shared 'Highland Spirit'.

Celebrating Highland dress

The Highland Society of London was dedicated to reviving Highland dress, which was still subject to the legal restrictions imposed in the aftermath of the last Jacobite rising. In 1782, the Society succeeded in having the laws on dress repealed in parliament. Freedom to wear Highland dress without fear of fine, imprisonment or transportation was restored across Scotland.

Highland dress represented all that the literary and artistic world saw as romantic about Scotland. Clubs and societies offered prizes for the best-dressed Highlanders at their piping and dance competitions, and set an early standard for Scotland's national costume.

During the early 19th century, the Highland Society of London compiled information about the traditional patterns of tartan worn by the chiefs and heads of families. Out of these efforts, the idea of clan tartans exclusively associated with specific family names emerged.

Below: Dress button (detail)

This engraved button is on a tartan dress coat associated with the Ancient Caledonian Society of London, which was founded to celebrate and promote the use of Highland dress.

Members of Highland clubs and societies often commissioned dress buttons to wear at meetings and on special occasions. The buttons typically carried a Gaelic motto or bore symbols of Scottish significance. They communicated the patriotism of the wearer, as well as their membership of a specific organisation.

Date of tartan dress coat, c.1786. On loan from The Scottish Tartans Authority. Image © National Museums Scotland

Right: Tartan suit (right)

This three-piece suit of Prince Charles Edward tartan features a set of gold-plated buttons embossed with the Gaelic phrase 'Comun nan Gael', meaning 'the Highland Society'.

Buttons on suit made by Hammond, Turner & Dickenson, c.1830, National Museums Scotland

Performing Scottishness

The Highland clubs and societies were determined to reverse the decline in the use of the Gaelic language and to revive distinctive aspects of Gaelic culture. They supported efforts to document and popularise bagpipe music, to record ancient folk tales, and to publish songs and poetry in Gaelic.

The Highland Society of London and the Highland Society of Scotland conducted their own public investigations into the controversy over James Macpherson's Ossian poetry. They concluded that the poems were indeed based on genuine Gaelic oral traditions, at least in part.

Piping competitions organised by Highland clubs and societies stimulated interest in Gaelic music. Local trading fairs became a focus for bagpiping and dance performances. By the first decades of the 19th century, music and dance featured alongside sporting competitions in the earliest formal Highland games, which revived the idea of traditional clan gatherings.

St Fillan's Highland Games

Organised Highland Games based on traditional clan gatherings emerged as a popular pastime in the early 19th century. Competitors took part in athletic events which required skill, stamina and strength, and vied for prizes in piping, singing and dancing.

From *Scotland illustrated in a series of eighty views from drawings*, by various Scottish artists, *c.*1850, written by Professor Wilson, National Museums Scotland

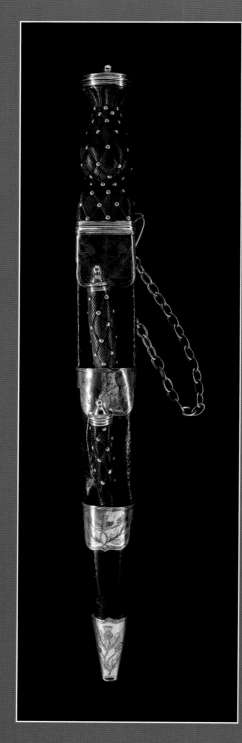

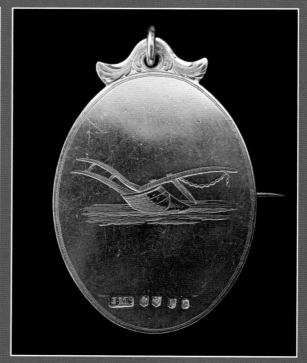

Left: Prize dirk

The winners of events at Highland Games often received traditional Highland dress accoutrements as prizes. This dirk was awarded to Charles Duff – the second best player of the Great Highland Bagpipe at a games organised by a Highland Friendly Society in 1826.

*c.*1826, National Museums Scotland

Above: Silver medal awarded to David Croll by the Highland Society of Scotland

As well as supporting Highland Games, some societies held annual competitions to promote changes in land use. Medals were awarded for demonstrations of new agricultural techniques, for undertaking specific improvements, or for long service to the Society.

*c.*1811–12, National Museums Scotland

From chiefs to landlords

The activities of the clubs and societies included efforts to improve the economic conditions of the Highlands and Islands. They promoted the establishment of new towns and villages, the building of roads and bridges, the reform of agriculture and fisheries, and the growth of trade and small industries.

Membership of the clubs and societies was drawn largely from the landed gentry. Economic change had profound consequences for many of their tenants, including those who found themselves removed by landlords in the name of agricultural progress. The measures now known to history as the Highland Clearances divided opinion amongst the members of the societies.

The clubs and societies faced a paradox. Their efforts to preserve Highland culture took effect while rapid modernisation was casting traditional ways of life aside. By outwardly celebrating the clan society of the past, Highland elites were stressing their traditional identities as chieftains. However, the economic reality was that they had become landlords first and foremost.

Map of Thurso farms, published in the appendix to 'An Account of the Improvements carried on by Sir John Sinclair, Bart, on his Estates in Scotland'

Sir John Sinclair of Ulbster established the town of Thurso in an attempt to generate new industry for tenants displaced from his estates in Caithness by changes in land use. The scheme did not prosper due to the area's isolated position and high transport costs. Some of the tenants were forced to emigrate as a result.

1812. Courtesy of www.ambaile.org.uk

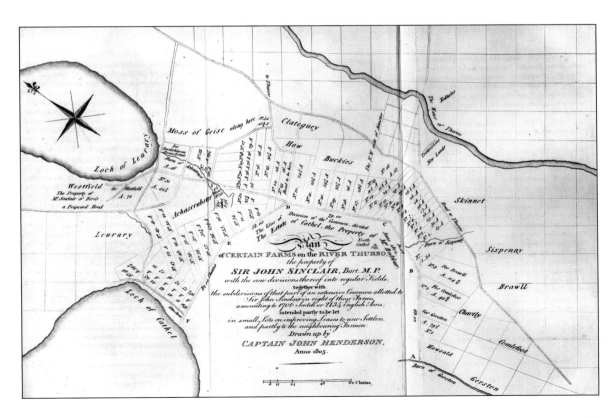

***Jane Maxwell, Duchess of Gordon (c.1749–1812), wife of the 4th Duke of Gordon, with her son George Duncan (1770–1836), Marquis of Huntly, later 5th Duke of Gordon* [detail]**

Jane, Duchess of Gordon, was credited with introducing tartan to London society. In 1792 she sent a sample of Black Watch tartan to China to be woven in the finest silk, which she then had made into a dress. Her son, George, Marquis of Huntly, commanded the 92nd Highlanders until 1799.

By George Romney (1734–1802), 1778, oil on canvas, Scottish National Portrait Gallery. Purchased 1972 with help from the Pilgrim Trust

40

From rebels to heroes

Clubs and societies celebrated the growing military reputation of the Highland regiments of the British army. In the late 18th century, mass recruitment for Britain's long wars against France was presented as evidence of the loyalty and heroism of Highlanders in the service of the state.

In 1801, British forces won a famous victory over Napoleonic France in Egypt. Highland regiments played a conspicuous role in the campaign. Afterwards, images of Highland soldiers in their picturesque uniforms became popular symbols of Scotland's contribution to British military success.

By 1815, Highland soldiers were widely celebrated as romantic icons of the British army with a reputation for bravery and sacrifice. Their victories in battles such as Alexandria, Vimeiro and Waterloo were represented as the latest chapter in a heroic history that stretched back centuries.

Left: Trophy presented to the 42nd Highlanders by the Highland Society of London

The Highland Society of London presented this trophy to the 42nd Highlanders in 1817, when it was filled with whisky as a toast to the regiment's military achievements. The cost of the gift – 120 guineas – was a significant investment, reflecting the extent to which the Society wished to celebrate Highland regiments.

By William Walker, c.1801–1805, The Black Watch Castle and Museum

Right: Sketch for medal

Many early designs for the medal commemorating the 42nd Highlanders were rejected. The sketch chosen was drawn by the celebrated painter Benjamin West, the president of the Royal Academy, who presented the subject of the drawing as both the 'Caledonian Hero' and a 'modern Achilles'.

By Benjamin West (1738–1820), 1801–25, pencil on paper, The Black Watch Castle and Museum

Highland style

The romantic image of the Highland soldier brought tartan clothing to the forefront of public attention. By the early 19th century, Highland military style had influenced civilian fashion on a grand scale.

The weaving company William Wilson & Sons of Bannockburn was at the heart of the revived tartan industry in Scotland. Founded in Stirlingshire in the 1760s, Wilsons was a key supplier of regimental tartans to soldiers serving at home and abroad. As Highland clubs and societies sought to preserve and promote tartan, Wilsons' cloth gained a wide reputation for quality and style.

Wilsons' tartans became highly fashionable, used in the tailoring of men's kilt suits, women's gowns, cloaks and children's clothing. Responding to this sharp increase in civilian consumer demand, the company became one of the most successful of the new commercial tartan weavers in Britain.

Below: Manufacturer's label attached to a sample of Campbell of Breadalbane tartan

Produced by Wilsons of Bannockburn, c.1860, © The Scottish Tartans Authority

Opposite: Letter from David Hadden to Wilsons of Bannockburn

By the 1820s, tartan was being exported across the world. Writing from New York in 1824, this merchant stated that red and green tartans were favoured by his customers. In particular, the Colquhoun, McDuff, Bruce, McKenzie and Glenorchy patterns were in high demand.

7 December 1824, New York, National Museums Scotland

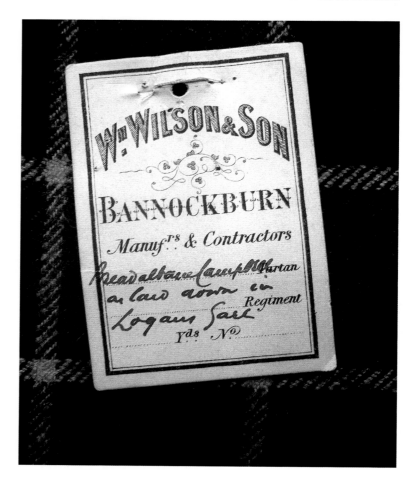

Glenorchy? Colquhoun & Stewart

Tartans for United States of America

15

Bannockburn   New York 7 Decr 1824

Messrs Wm Wilson & Son

Dear Sirs

Tartans continue in fair demand & as you may be preparing some I think I had better send you a few patts of the patterns most esteemed - the best of all is the Colquhoun of a very large size as inclosed patt. & nearly one half shd be like it some with silk & some without there is another inclosed patt with a Red Stripe which is good - if you charge them all one price you should tell me the relative value of the different qualities & of those with & without silk & you should send me patts of your goods in a parcell & then I can sell them common without opening them - the McDuff & Bruce are also good patts & so the McKenzie & Glenorchy & generally speaking the

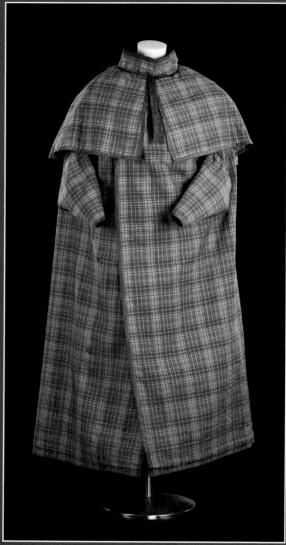

Tiered cloak

This tiered cloak is made from Royal Stewart tartan – one of the most recognisable tartan patterns. It first became fashionable with the general public during the early 19th century, thanks to its use by members of the British royal family. It is fully lined with bright printed cotton and fastens at the neck by gold clasps in the shape of lion's paws.

*c.*1820, National Museums Scotland

Woman's caped cloak

This caped cloak is tailored from one of the earliest known examples of the Buchanan tartan. This version of the sett was woven by Wilsons of Bannockburn in the early 19th century. During this period, the pattern was sold as a fashion fabric and not as a clan tartan.

    The cloak is practical, yet elegant. An interior drawstring allows the cape to be synched at the upper back, which would have complemented the high-waisted fashions worn by women at the time.

*c.*1800–10, National Museums Scotland

Augusta, Duchess of Cambridge (1797–1889), with Prince George (1819–1904) and Princess Augusta of Cambridge (1822–1916)

In this group portrait Prince George is wearing a tartan kilt dress. It is made from Prince Charles Edward tartan. This pattern was named to take advantage of the growing popular interest in the lost Jacobite cause and was sold by Wilsons of Bannockburn throughout the 19th century.

By Melchoir Gommar Tieleman (1784–1864), 1823, oil on canvas, Royal Collection Trust / © Her Majesty Queen Elizabeth II 2019

Royal favour

The romantic captivation with Scotland soon reached the British monarchy. Though Jacobite clans had fought to overthrow their dynasty, by the end of the 18th century the House of Hanover no longer regarded Highlanders with suspicion. Members of the royal household collected Highland weaponry, joined Highland societies, and commissioned elaborate outfits of Highland dress.

Royal interest in Scotland was typified by the visit of King George IV to Edinburgh in 1822. A programme of events was carefully managed by the author Sir Walter Scott and historian Colonel David Stewart of Garth.

The visit took place at a time of industrial unrest in urban Scotland, and of economic crisis in the Highlands and Islands. In contrast, the pageantry surrounding the visit was laden with tartan and idealised representations of Highland clanship.

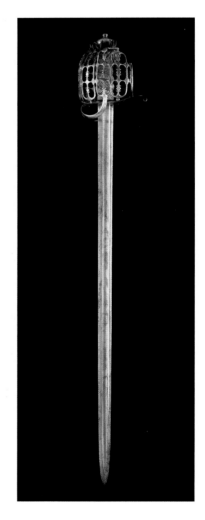

Right: Backsword belonging to Prince Frederick, Duke of York and Albany

The royal family maintained an interest in traditional Highland culture even as clan society became increasingly associated with rebellion. Throughout the 18th century the royal princes in London acquired Highland weapons and were given instruction on how to use them by Highland officers in the British army.

Late 18th century, National Museums Scotland

Opposite: Jaguar skin dress sporran with the badge of the Order of the Thistle, and a kilt of Earl of Inverness tartan, belonging to Prince Augustus Frederick

Prince Augustus Frederick, known in Scotland as the Earl of Inverness, was a significant royal patron of romantic Highland culture during the early 19th century. The Prince was a leading member of the Highland Society of London and commanded the Loyal North Britons volunteers. Throughout his lifetime he amassed an impressive collection of Highland costume and weaponry.

Sporran c.1805, kilt c.1815. On loan from The Scottish Tartans Authority. Image © National Museums Scotland

'One and twenty daft days'

When King George IV visited Edinburgh in 1822 it was the first time a reigning monarch had set foot in Scotland since the coronation of King Charles II in 1651.

The King's Scottish tour was modelled on a state visit to Dublin in 1821, which had aimed to inspire Irish loyalty to the United Kingdom of Great Britain and Ireland. The King was not popular with the public and the tours were seen as one way to restore his failing reputation. The visit to Edinburgh

Below: *George IV landing at Leith, 1822*

This painting recreates the multitude of spectators who came to witness the King arriving at Leith on 15 August 1822.

By Alexander Carse (*c.*1770–1843), 1822, oil on canvas. Photograph credit: City of Edinburgh Council

suited British politicians who sought to keep the King away from the Congress of Verona, where the political future of Europe was being decided.

The visit was a moment of intense symbolism, one which was intended to signal reconciliation and Scotland's loyalty to the British royal family.

It also demonstrated that Scotland retained a distinct national character, while still being part of the United Kingdom.

Planning a Highland spectacle

Anticipating King George IV's desire for a great Highland spectacle, the celebrated writer Sir Walter Scott and the soldier and historian Colonel David Stewart of Garth were placed in charge of organising the visit. Both men were regarded as authorities on the history and culture of Scotland.

Scott and Stewart masterminded a programme of patriotic events that championed Scotland's loyalty to the Crown, with a strong Highland flavour. Prior to the visit, Scott circulated a pamphlet encouraging the citizens of Edinburgh to adopt Highland dress and to wear blue and white cockades as badges of national pride.

By staging the visit in a manner that celebrated the shared nature of Scotland's feudal past, the organisers hoped to heal the social and political divisions of the country. Their aim was to bring all Scots together beneath a banner of romantic sentiment.

Highland suit worn by William Blackhall

Born in Haddington, William Blackhall was one of those Lowlanders who adopted the romantic style of Highland dress advocated by Sir Walter Scott.

*c.*1822, National Museums Scotland

A controversial event

The royal visit attracted much controversy and critics complained that a romanticised ideal of Highland history had been imposed upon the whole of Scotland. Some observed that the celebration of tartan, tradition and calls to clanship were inappropriate at a time of social and economic turmoil in the Highlands.

Despite Sir Walter Scott's invitation, relatively few heads of Highland families attended the festivities. As Lowland Scots donned Highland dress and paraded through the streets of Edinburgh, commentators questioned the authenticity of the proceedings.

The most vocal of these critics was the Chief of Glengarry, Alasdair Ranaldson MacDonell, who had formed his own Society of True Highlanders in 1815. Glengarry was interested in preserving what he considered to be a purer version of Highland traditions, with a strong emphasis on ancestry and the Gaelic language. He clashed repeatedly with Sir Walter Scott and Colonel David Stewart of Garth throughout the visit.

An incident during the visit of George IV to Edinburgh, 1822

This hurried sketch of six unidentified men, portrays the various costumes worn by attendees during the royal visit. The four central figures wear Highland dress and carry traditional Highland weaponry, including pistols, dirks, broadswords, and a targe. They are accompanied by a member of the Royal Company of Archers and a man in military uniform.

By Sir David Wilkie (1785–1841), 1822, pencil and watercolour on paper, Scottish National Portrait Gallery

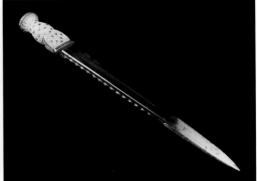

Above: Dirk

This dirk can be clearly seen on the portrait of Glengarry painted by Sir Henry Raeburn (left).

Owned by MacDonell of Glengarry (1771–1828), Museum of the Isles, Armadale Castle, Isle of Skye

Above: Quaich

This traditional quaich, or drinking vessel, celebrates King George IV's visit to Edinburgh.

Owned by MacDonell of Glengarry (1771–1828), 1822, Museum of the Isles, Armadale Castle, Isle of Skye

Right: Colonel Alasdair Ranaldson MacDonell of Glengarry (1771–1828) [detail]

Sir Henry Raeburn's painting depicts Glengarry as the quintessential Highland chief – wearing full Highland dress in the archaic setting of an old baronial hall, with a Highland targe and broadswords hanging on the wall. While maintaining this traditional image, Glengarry was one of those who was criticised for clearing tenants from his estates.

By Sir Henry Raeburn (1756–1823), c.1812, oil on canvas, National Galleries of Scotland

Alasdair Ranaldson MacDonell of Glengarry (1771–1828)

Glengarry felt that he should play a central role in the royal visit, not only as chief of an ancient and powerful clan but also as the head of a society of Highland gentlemen. Sir Walter Scott did not allow a place for Glengarry's Society of True Highlanders in the official celebrations, but the chieftain managed to impose himself on the royal procession, riding forward uninvited to welcome the King to Scotland.

Gaelic voices

The proud plaid

When the men of the short kilts
Go in battle-order, loud will be heard
Deadly airs from roar of pipe drones
Underscoring chanters' shrieking.

John Mackintosh, *Song to Glengarry*, 1822

Ever on the lookout for an opportunity to garner self-publicity, and scandalised by the sight of hordes of Lowlanders in Highland dress, Alasdair Ranaldson MacDonell, the proud chief of Glengarry, is said to have used King George IV's visit to Edinburgh in 1822 to issue a challenge. As celebrated by the bard John Mackintosh, the best soldiers, armed with musket and bayonet, were invited to fight against an equal number of his own clansmen with broadsword and targe. Perhaps fortunately for the men of Glengarry, the challenge was not accepted.

For many landlords and gentlemen, the new fashion for Highland dress, with its rules, restrictions and mystique, lent chiefs an exotic glamour, handy for cutting a dash in the outside world. This colourful image was often at odds with the poverty endured by many of their tenants.

Guthan nan Gàidheal

Am breacan uallach

Nuair thèid luchd nam fèiltean geàrr'
An òrdugh blàir gur h-àrd a chluinntear,
Toirmrich dhos nam porta bàsmhor,
Cumail beus ri gàirich shiunnsair.

Iain Mac an Tòisich, *Òran do Mhac 'ic Alasdair*, 1822

Bha Alasdair MacDhòmhnaill, Mac Mhic Alasdair Ghleann Garadh, a-riamh airson aire dhaoine a tharraing thuige fhèin. Ri linn cuairt an Rìgh gu Dùn Èideann ann an 1822, ghabh an ceann-cinnidh tàmailt leis na treudan de Ghoill fo èideadh breacain. A rèir a' bhàird Iain Mac an Tòisich, thug e seachad dùbhlan: sabaid eadar na saighdearan dearga a b' fheàrr, le musgaidean agus beuglaidean, agus àireamh cho-ionnan den chinneadh Ghàidhealach aige fhèin, le claidheamhan agus targaidean. Nach buidhe do dh'fhir Ghleann Garadh nach deach gabhail ris!

Do dh'iomadach duine-uasal, bha am fasan ùr airson breacan nan Gàidheal, le riaghailtean àraid agus romansachas na lùib, a' toirt àrd-inbhe agus eireachdas do na cinn-chinnidh. Chuir iad seo gu deagh bhuil anns an t-saoghal a-muigh. Ach ged a bha coltas lìomhte leòmach air na daoine mòra, 's tric a bha na daoine beaga a' fulang bochdainn agus fòirneart.

Parades and pageantry

The royal visit of 1822 was marked by extravagant parades, balls, banquets and ceremonies. Attendees dressed to impress, alternating between Highland dress, military uniforms, and costumes in the blue and white colours of Scotland's patron saint, St Andrew. Not all the pageantry was given a Highland character. Sir Walter Scott emphasised Scotland's status as an ancient kingdom by introducing the medieval crown, sceptre and sword of state into the ceremonies.

For the festivities, Highland aristocrats reverted to their role of ancient clan chiefs. Some attended with groups of retainers drawn from their estates. They dressed in Highland costumes and carried traditional weapons, often made or adapted for the occasion.

For many, the abiding memory of the royal visit was the appearance of King George himself wearing Highland dress and being greeted by a tartan-wearing population. The King's critics were quick to make fun of the whole event.

Left: *Patrick Grant [Pàdraig Grannd an Dubh-bhruaich] (1713/14–1824)*

Colvin Smith produced this portrait of Patrick Grant in June 1822, when the sitter was 109. Grant, also known as the 'Highland Patriarch', was believed to be the last survivor of the Battle of Culloden. He had fought on the side of the Jacobite army in 1746, but was offered a generous pension by King George IV as an act of reconciliation and respect for his 'oldest enemy'.

The Highland dress worn by Grant was provided for him by the artist in order to make the portrait more in keeping with the expectations of an audience increasingly aware of the romantic dimensions of Scottish history.

By Colvin Smith (1795–1875), 1822, oil on canvas, Scottish National Portrait Gallery

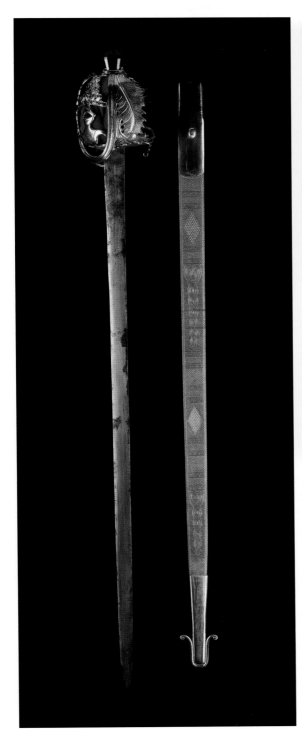

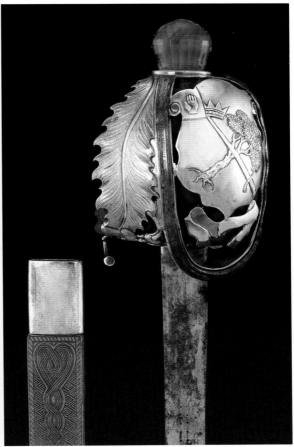

Left and right (detail): Highland dress sword, worn by Sir Evan John Murray-MacGregor

This sword was originally a family heirloom of the MacGregors. An inscription on the blade records that it was carried by a MacGregor during the 1745 Jacobite rising, and claims that it was cut down from a sword carried in battle in 1602. The weapon was remodelled in preparation for the royal visit, incorporating a decorated silver basket hilt.

*c.*1822, National Museums Scotland. Acquired with the aid of the Art Fund. Image © National Museums Scotland

Opposite, right: Wine glass

This glass, engraved with royal crown and thistle motifs, may have been used at a banquet given in the King's honour at Parliament House, Edinburgh, on 24 August 1822.

*c.*1822, National Museums Scotland

A tour of Scotland

My journey through the Highlands was perfectly inspiring, and I hope I have laid in a good stock of new poetical ideas from it …

Robert Burns, 1787

From the late 18th century, romantic inclinations towards dramatic locations and places of solitude drew visitors to Scotland in increasing numbers. Tourists were especially attracted to locations depicted in Romantic paintings, prints and literature.

Highland sporting estates provided a playground for wealthy folk who could afford to escape from city life. The rapid building of railways from the 1840s made it easier for tourists to seek out the experiences they craved.

For many tourists, Scotland represented a journey into a heightened sense of the past. Visitors were less aware of the realities of the carefully managed environment of large Highland estates, or of the pressing concerns of the people who lived there.

Inspiring journeys

Writers, artists and musicians were among the tourists who visited Scotland in pursuit of the romantic experience. Often they were on a personal pilgrimage inspired by the lasting influence of James Macpherson's Ossian poetry, or the fame of other Scottish writers such as Robert Burns and Sir Walter Scott.

These celebrity visitors created their own works of art, inspired by the places they had visited, often composed in situ. Works by major figures, including Dorothy and William Wordsworth, JMW Turner and Felix Mendelssohn inspired more people to seek out the places evoked in music, art and literature for themselves.

Scotland became a source of romantic inspiration for many people who never visited in person. Traditional Scottish music, folk tales, stories from Ossian and Scott's novels and poetry, all became popular subjects for European artists, authors and composers who journeyed to Scotland only in their imagination.

Felix Mendelssohn

Felix Mendelssohn (1809–47) was a German Romantic composer. His tour of Scotland in 1829 inspired one of his most celebrated compositions, the concert overture *The Hebrides*.

Mendelssohn left London on 24 July and arrived in Edinburgh four days later. After a brief stop in Melrose to visit Sir Walter Scott, Mendelssohn embarked for the Highlands and Islands. He travelled through Perthshire to Fort William before visiting the islands of Mull and Staffa and returning south via Glasgow.

60

Above: Sketchbook

On 2 August 1829, Mendelssohn visited Ossian's Hall, a folly overlooking the Falls of Braan near Dunkeld, Perthshire – a popular tourist attraction that allowed visitors to view the spectacular sights and sounds of a Highland waterfall surrounded by painted depictions of scenes from Ossian.

By Felix Mendelssohn (1809–47), 1829, The Bodleian Libraries, University of Oxford

Right: Original score of *The Hebrides* concert overture

It is often suggested that Mendelssohn's overture *The Hebrides* was inspired by his trip to Fingal's Cave, island of Staffa. In fact, he composed the music before that trip, being 'extraordinarily affected' by the sights travelling from Fort William to Mull.

By Felix Mendelssohn (1809–47), The Bodleian Libraries, University of Oxford

61

Gaelic voices

At a distance

There were many toffs down on the quarter-deck of the ship –
English folk, Lowlanders, and French folk – some eating, some
sleeping, some yawning. One of them had a long, fancy telescope
to his eye, as if he was going to fire at Duart Castle …
    I took out the bagpipe as requested, but at the first blast they
all fled apart from one big fat Englishman, who sat opposite me
with his fingers in his ears, scowling as if I were going to eat him.

Rev Norman MacLeod,
writing as 'Finlay the Piper' in *The Gaelic Messenger*, 1829

Not all travellers thronging the Highlands were outsiders. Educated Gaels
from the east of the region made their own personal pilgrimages to the
west, curious to observe what they saw as a primitive way of life and keen
to collect the traditional culture of their ancestors before progress extin-
guished it.

Writers from the Highlands acted as cultural brokers for outside
audiences eager to read thrilling stories about bloodthirsty clans and
outlandish superstitions. Other Gaels found work in the growing tourist
and sporting markets as hosts, ghillies, stalkers, and local guides ready,
for a price, with romantic Gaelic songs and tall tales. On island steamers,
tartan-clad bagpipers played to the tourists to announce meal-times, and
arranged impromptu dances on deck.

Guthan nan Gàidheal

Fad air astar

Bha mòran uaislean shìos air clàr-dheiridh na luinge – Sasannaich, Goill agus Frangaich – cuid dhiubh a' leughadh; cuid nan codal; cuid a' mèananaich; cuid ag itheadh. Bha fear dhiubh le gloin'-amhairc fhada rìomhach r'a shùil, mar gum biodh e a' dol a losgadh air Caisteal Dubhairt …

Thug mi fhèin a mach na pìob mar a dh' iarr; ach a' chiad sgal a thug i, theich gach aon dhiùbh ach aon Sasannach mòr, reamhar, a shuidh mum choinne le 'dhà mheur na 'chluasan, agus sgraing air mar gum bithinn a' dol ga itheadh.

An t-Urr. Tormod MacLeòid, a' sgrìobhadh mar 'Fhionnlagh Pìobaire' anns *An Teachdaire Gaelach*, 1829

Cha b' iad coigrich a-mhàin a chaidh air chuairt don taobh tuath. Chaidh Gàidheil fhoghlaimte bho thaobh sear na Gàidhealtachd air eilthireachd don taobh siar airson beachdachadh air dòigh-bheatha a bha, nan sùilean-san, aosmhor àrsaidh, agus airson dualchas an cuid sinnsireachd a chruinneachadh mus cuireadh linn ùr às dha.

Bha sgrìobhaichean às a' Ghàidhealtachd mar eadar-mheadhan cultarach do dhaoine air an taobh a-muigh. Dh'aithris iad sgeulachdan iongantach mu chinnidhean borba agus cleachdaidhean annasach. Rinn Gàidheil eile am bith-beò ann an obair thurasachd agus shealgaireachd, mar ostairean, stalcairean, agus luchd-iùil a ghabhadh òrain romansach agus a dh'innseadh naidheachdan neònach – airson duais bheag. Air na bàtaichean-smùid, chluicheadh pìobairean ann am breacan don luchd-turais aig àm lòin, agus airson dannsaichean air deic a chuireadh seachad an tìde dhaibh.

Sir Walter Scott

The poetry and novels of Sir Walter Scott brought some of Scotland's evocative landscapes to public attention across Britain and Europe. Loch Katrine in Stirlingshire is the fictional setting of Scott's poem 'The Lady of the Lake', published in 1810. The poem inspired many tourists to visit the loch and see for themselves the romantic places described by Scott.

Right: Table centrepiece

This silver table centrepiece is decorated with scenes from Scott's epic 'The Lady of the Lake'. It was made in Edinburgh in c.1880, possibly to mark the 70th anniversary of the poem's publication in 1810.

By Mackay, Cunningham and Co., Edinburgh, c.1880–81, National Museums Scotland

Opposite: Furnishing fabric

This fabric depicts scenes from Scott's poem 'The Lady of the Lake'. It was made in Nantes in France by the renowned fabric manufacturers Favre-Petitpierre et cie.

Made by Favre-Petitpierre et cie, c.1825, National Museums Scotland

Hunting, shooting and fishing

During the final decades of the 18th century, classical mansion houses were built across the Highlands, as the old defensive architecture of clanship gave way to the polite tastes of the landed gentry. Highland landowners embraced active lifestyles built on the notion of conquering the outdoors, which they related to the traditional hunting pursuits of their ancestors.

From the 1830s, a growing enthusiasm amongst tourists for deerstalking, grouse shooting and salmon fishing prompted estate owners to rent out their land during the sporting seasons. Large areas of the Highlands were turned into an exclusive playground for wealthy visitors based in a network of newly built, romantically-fashioned shooting lodges.

Like the sheep farms which had dominated Highland landscapes since the late 18th century, the sporting estates operated in large empty spaces that had often been cleared of people. What appeared like a romantic wilderness was really an artificial, closely managed environment.

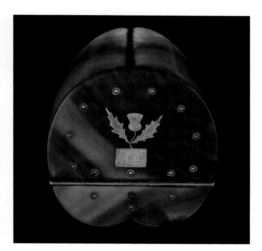

Right: *Scene in the Highlands, with portraits of the Duchess of Bedford, the Duke of Gordon and Lord Alexander Russell* [detail]

Landscape painter Sir Edwin Landseer was one of the most renowned Romantic artists of the 19th century. This painting depicts Landseer's patron, George, 5th Duke of Gordon, with his sister, Georgiana, the Duchess of Bedford, and her son.

By Edwin Landseer (1802–73), *c.*1825–28, oil on canvas. Private Collection, on loan to the National Galleries of Scotland

Above: Snuff box

Taking snuff was a popular gentlemanly pursuit. This snuff box is made from a deer's hoof and was the property of Donald Macdonald of Dalchosnie.

Mid-19th century, National Museums Scotland

Fragments of the landscape

From the mid-18th century, Scottish crystals and agates known simply as 'pebbles' were made into pieces of jewellery that were popular with tourists as souvenirs. The owners of these pieces could keep and wear their own small portion of the natural beauty of Scotland.

Scottish freshwater pearls come in many colours – white, pinks, greys and browns. Such imperfections and colourings symbolised their rarity and natural origins. The use of these pearls in jewellery fluctuated, as periods of overfishing affected supply, and demand was especially high in the late 18th century and from the 1860s.

High demand for these small luxuries created new industries linking rural places with town craftsmen. Agates collected on the shores of the Isle of Rum were sold on to specialist workers called lapidaries in Edinburgh, who cut and polished them into fashionable curiosities.

By the mid-19th century, jewellers and lapidaries were creating elaborate mosaics referencing different places. During the 1860s, a 'gold rush' in Sutherland drew renewed attention to Scotland's rich mineralogy.

Left: Brooch of Scottish gold, cairngorm crystal and Scottish freshwater pearls

A showcase of materials sourced in the Scottish landscape, this piece fuses metals, stone and pearls.

By Muirhead & Son, Glasgow, *c.*1869, National Museums Scotland

Right: Agate brooch set in silver

Simple shapes framed with subtle sparkle emphasised the patterns of the natural stone. They were worn as jewellery and displayed in curiosity cabinets as geological specimens, marking the owner's knowledge of landscape and mineralogy. Collecting and wearing pebbles enabled women to engage in scientific interests that were considered the preserve of men.

19th century, National Museums Scotland

Agate or 'Scotch pebble'

In their raw form, agates or 'Scotch pebbles' look
unremarkable, but cut open they reveal different
colours and patterns that were viewed as miniature
pictures of the Scottish landscape.

From Monifieth, Angus, National Museums Scotland

Background: *Loch Awe, Argyll and Bute*

The artist Horatio McCulloch captured the picturesque
ruins of Kilchurn Castle against the backdrop of Ben
Lui, an inspirational Romantic landscape which had
been the subject of a painting by JMW Turner some
thirty years before. Kilchurn Castle was the home of
the Campbells of Glenorchy, the most powerful branch
of Clan Campbell, who held large estates in Argyll and
the central Highlands.

Some of McCulloch's landscapes were engraved for
illustrations in topographical books and would have
been familiar to many tourists to the Highlands and
Islands.

By Horatio McCulloch (1805–67), *c.*1850, oil on
canvas, University of Aberdeen

It is now become fashionable among the English to make a tour into Scotland for some weeks or months ...

The Weekly Magazine, 1772

The Gothic revival

During the 19th century romantic tastes increasingly turned to Gothic art, architecture and literature inspired by medieval history. This was a Europe-wide phenomenon and one which complemented a growing sense of nationalism emerging across the continent.

In Scotland, there was renewed interest in heroic events from the medieval period. The poetry of Robert Burns had re-ignited interest in the history of the Wars of Independence of the 13th and 14th centuries. The patriotic deeds of Sir William Wallace and Robert the Bruce were celebrated in popular culture.

Elite Highlanders adapted Gothic fashion by linking Highland culture to a chivalric interpretation of the medieval past. When the Earl of Eglinton staged a mock medieval tournament in Ayrshire in 1839, one Highland aristocrat attended as 'The Knight of the Gael'. He wore authentic medieval armour and was supported by his retinue of Highland clansmen, the Atholl Highlanders.

Opposite, above: '*Viscount Glenlyon as the Knight of the Gael, followed by the men of Athol*'

The costumes of Viscount Glenlyon and his retinue of Atholl Highlanders were second in extravagance only to the Earl of Eglinton. Glenlyon's chosen role as Knight of the Gael was an attempt to reconcile the traditions of Highland Romanticism with the growing fashion for the medieval.

By Hugh Wilson, after Charles Achille d'Hardiviller, 1839, National Museums Scotland

Opposite, below: Helmet with the 'Wild Man of Atholl' crest

This helmet was part of the suit of armour worn by Viscount Glenlyon in his character as the Knight of the Gael. The 'Wild Man of Atholl' is a heraldic crest associated with the Murrays of Atholl. Viscount Glenlyon became the 6th Duke of Atholl in 1846.

Helmet c.1560, crest added c.1839. On loan from Blair Castle Collection, Perthshire. Image © National Museums Scotland

The Eglinton Tournament

On 30 August 1839, the Earl of Eglinton hosted a re-enactment of a medieval tournament at his castle in Ayrshire. Over 100,000 spectators turned out to watch the spectacle. The tournament was inspired by the chivalric ideals of Gothic Revival, which drew on tales of honour and bravery from the middle ages. Many of the tournament's features were based on Sir Walter Scott's 1819 novel *Ivanhoe*.

The knights who competed at the Eglinton Tournament were Scottish aristocrats and gentlemen. They wore family heirlooms or procured antique armour, decorated with heraldic crests. It later transpired that some pieces of armour purchased for the occasion were in fact 19th-century replicas.

Plaid brooch

Silver plaid brooch set with a cairngorm and a ring of 16 carbuncles, worn by the chiefs of Clanranald.

Mid-19th century, National Museums Scotland

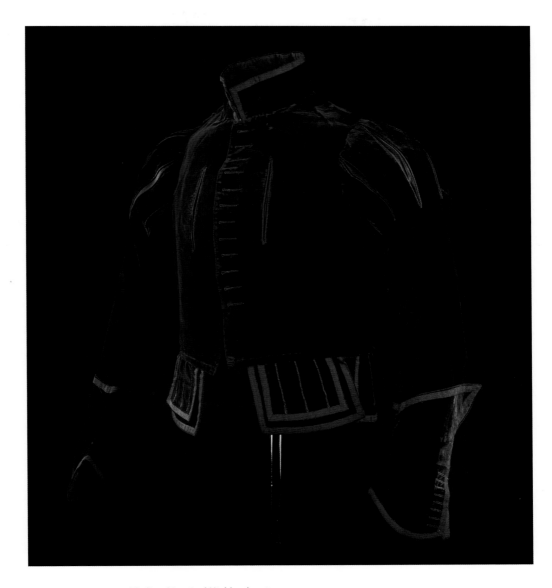

Medieval-inspired Highland costume

During the early Victorian period, there was a fashion among the British aristocracy for historically-themed costume balls and re-enactments. Guests at these events wore 'ancient' national costumes or dressed as notable historical figures, often inspired by authentic illustrations from medieval manuscripts.

Growing interest in a romantic, medieval past influenced the style of Highland dress. This blue velvet coat with slashed sleeves and gauntlet cuffs, and the jewelled plaid brooch on the opposite page, belonged to Ranald George Macdonald, 20th Chief of Clanranald.

Mid-19th century, National Museums Scotland

Sentimental Jacobitism

By the Victorian period, romantic memory of the Jacobite wars of the previous century could be indulged without trace of an active political agenda. The 'lost cause' of Prince Charles Edward Stuart and his Jacobite army, and the pursuit of the fugitive Prince through the Highlands by British soldiers, were raised to mythological status as part of Scotland's national story.

The centenary of the last Jacobite rising in 1845 increased popular interest. New generations were nostalgic for an era which contrasted with Scotland's increasingly industrialised society. The Jacobite story embodied values of chivalry, heroism and the unfailing loyalty of the Highlanders to their exiled Prince and his doomed enterprise.

This yearning for a noble past rooted in traditional clan society was quite detached from the reality of modern life in Scotland, yet the songs and stories of the Jacobite wars lived on as a powerful memory in Gaelic culture.

Carved wooden picture frame, containing a print titled *Prince Charles Edward and the Highlanders entering Edinburgh after the Battle of Prestonpans*

This intricately carved wooden frame contains a mid-19th century print, which shows the Jacobite army entering Edinburgh in September 1745. The frame was commissioned by the Macpherson family in 1845 to commemorate the centenary of the last Jacobite rising.

The frame features recognisable Highland and Jacobite symbols, such as Prince Charles Edward Stuart's medusa-headed targe, now on display in the National Museum of Scotland. The Macdonald and Macpherson coats of arms decorate each side of the frame, reinforcing the clans' ancestral link to the Jacobite cause.

Print by Frederick Bacon, after Thomas Duncan, *c.*1845, National Museums Scotland

The Sobieski Stuarts

John and Charles Hay Allan, also known as the Sobieski Stuart brothers, were scholars of Highland dress, weaponry and Gaelic culture. Throughout the first half of the 19th century, they presented themselves as the sole surviving descendants of Prince Charles Edward Stuart. Though their claims of royal descent were fanciful, they enjoyed the patronage of Highland aristocrats who remained sentimentally attached to the lost cause of the Jacobites.

The brothers issued two books that claimed a medieval origin for clan tartan – the *Vestiarium Scoticum* in 1842 and *The Costume of the Clans* in 1845. The authenticity of the *Vestiarium Scoticum* has been widely questioned. It was based on a 16th-century manuscript of dubious origin, which the brothers never made available for public inspection.

The issue of the brothers' credibility obscured the diligent research on Highland history and culture which they undertook in various Gaelic sources.

The Highland ideal

There is a great peculiarity about the Highlands … a wildness, a liberty, and a solitude that had such a charm for us …

Queen Victoria, 1844

The mid-19th century saw a second wave of interest in Highland culture. Queen Victoria's affection for the Highlands and Islands as a place of happiness and solace kept the romantic vision of Scotland alive in the public imagination.

The Queen's domesticated, ordered version of an ideal past became fixed as the defining image of Scotland. Although romantic fashions changed during the period, this essential idea endured. It was an image which many ordinary Scots, including Highlanders, identified with strongly. And yet, during the Victorian period, the Highlands and Islands experienced periods of economic turmoil, emigration, agitation for land reform, and the continued decline of the Gaelic language.

Tartan dress, worn by Princess Victoria

As a young woman, Princess Victoria's impressions of Scotland were shaped by fashionable romantic culture. After reading Sir Walter Scott's historical novel *The Bride of Lammermoor* in 1836, the future monarch became a devotee of Scott and the romantic vision of Scotland presented in his work.

Silk velvets, woven to imitate tartan, were popular in both England and France during the early 19th century. This gown, trimmed with lace and silk tartan bows, would have been the height of fashionable taste for the young princess.

*c.*1835–37, Royal Collection Trust / © Her Majesty Queen Elizabeth II 2019

78

Prince Albert (1819–61)

Prince Albert often wore Highland dress when in Scotland. In this
miniature portrait, he is shown standing in a Highland landscape,
dressed in a Royal Stewart kilt. The matching plaid is fastened at the
shoulder with a large cairngorm brooch.

By Robert Thorburn (1818–85), 1852, watercolour on ivory, Royal
Collection Trust / © Her Majesty Queen Elizabeth II 2019

Royal tourists

The young Queen Victoria was captivated by the romantic idea of Scotland. Her interest was encouraged by her husband Prince Albert, who had grown up in a German aristocratic society that was itself steeped in romantic attitudes towards landscape, history and hunting. Both were avid readers of the poems and novels of Sir Walter Scott, and admired the paintings of artists such as Sir Edwin Landseer, which glorified Highland deerstalking.

In 1842, the royal couple visited Scotland for the first time. Their tour took them to some of the great aristocratic houses and shooting lodges of the Highlands. The grand reception that was arranged for them at Taymouth Castle mixed Highland Romanticism with a strong medieval theme, convincing the Queen and Prince Albert that they had discovered a magical kingdom within their own realm.

Further tours followed in 1844 and 1848, deepening the attachment of the Queen and Prince Albert to the aristocratic Highland lifestyle and leading them to search for a Highland residence of their own.

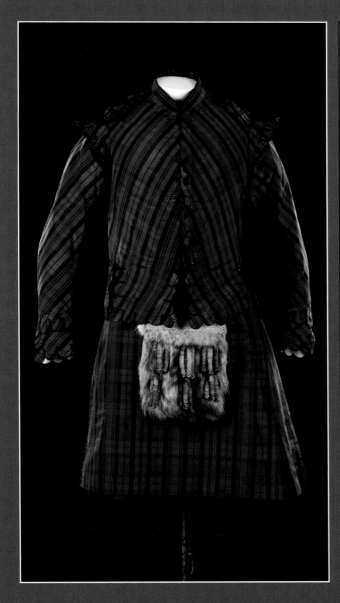

Highland dress costume

This costume is thought to have belonged to John Campbell, 2nd Marquis of Breadalbane, who entertained Queen Victoria at Taymouth Castle in September 1842. The jacket and kilt of this Highland dress costume are made from Black Watch silk tartan, immaculately tailored in a romantic medieval style. The small size and decoration of the sporran is characteristic of those worn with fancy dress.

*c.*1835–40, National Museums Scotland

Drummond silk tartan dress, worn by Lady Willoughby de Eresby

After leaving Taymouth, the royal party spent two nights at Drummond Castle. A lavish ball was held to mark the end of the Queen's stay. The hostess and 'Chieftainness of the Clan Drummond', Lady Willoughby de Eresby, wore this dress with a Highland bonnet of blue velvet, trimmed with eagle plumes, diamonds, and a sprig of holly. Her three daughters, Clementina, Elizabeth and Charlotte, also wore dresses of Drummond silk tartan.

*c.*1842, Highland Folk Museum, High Life Highland

Grand Gothic Hall at Taymouth Castle

This is one of a set of prints documenting Queen Victoria's tour of Scotland in 1842. When the royal party arrived at Taymouth Castle, they were greeted by the Marquis of Breadalbane and an honour guard of Highlanders from his estate. Pipers played, reels were danced, and bonfires were lit on the surrounding hills to celebrate the arrival of the monarch. The Queen was struck by this 'princely and romantic setting'. In her journal she noted that 'it seemed as if a great chieftain in olden feudal times was receiving his sovereign'. A grand ball was held to welcome the royal party, with the majority of gentlemen in attendance wearing elaborate outfits of Highland dress.

Andrew Maclure and Maclure & McDonald, 1843, Royal Collection Trust / © Her Majesty Queen Elizabeth II 2019

'This dear Paradise'

Evening at Balmoral Castle

Carl Haag's composition captures the return of Prince Albert from a successful stag hunt. He presents Queen Victoria with his kill, bathed in the torchlight of the surrounding ghillies, including John Brown in the centre foreground.

By Carl Haag (1820–1915), 1854, watercolour, Royal Collection Trust / © Her Majesty Queen Elizabeth II 2019

In 1848, Queen Victoria and Prince Albert leased the Balmoral sporting estate on the upper River Dee in the Aberdeenshire Highlands, a part of the country where the population had declined through emigration and where Gaelic was still widely spoken. The couple bought the property four years later and embarked on rebuilding Balmoral Castle as their ideal Highland home.

The new Balmoral was a grand homage to the romantic vision of Scotland, with fashionable Gothic touches. For the luxurious interiors, thistle motifs were incorporated into the wallpapers and tableware. Tartan was used in abundance in the carpets, curtains and upholstery. As the years passed, Prince Albert's growing collection of stags' head trophies was displayed in the halls and corridors.

Balmoral was a holiday refuge for the royal family, away from the pressures of public life, with accommodation for large parties of private and official guests. For the Queen it was her 'dear Paradise'.

The Balmoral lifestyle

The royal family's annual Balmoral visits were taken up with outdoor excursions through the surrounding mountains, attended by servants and estate workers. While Queen Victoria made sketches and paintings, Prince Albert hunted deer, attempted to learn Gaelic, and planned improvements to the estate.

In 1861, Prince Albert died unexpectedly. For the remainder of her reign, Queen Victoria mourned his death and insisted that life on the Balmoral estate be ritualistically preserved as he had known it. The Queen took comfort in the isolation of Balmoral and in her interactions with the estate staff, tenants and local population, whom she saw as following a simple, harmonious way of life.

Queen Victoria's attachment to her personal ideal of the Highlands gave a new lease of life to tourism based upon nostalgia and sentiment about the true nature of Scotland. The Balmoral formula of Highland dress, outdoor life, piping and Highland games, imposed a lasting structure on popular ideas about Scottish traditions.

Hunting double rifle

John Brown had worked on the Balmoral estate since 1842, and rose in the Queen's favour to special status as Her Majesty's Personal Servant. After Prince Albert's death in 1861, Brown supported Victoria in her grief. Gossip soon spread regarding the Queen's closeness to Brown and his influence over the royal household.

The gold plaque fitted into the butt of this rifle records that Queen Victoria presented it to John Brown as a Christmas gift in 1873. The high-quality design and obvious expense of the gift highlights the position of trust and esteem held by Brown.

By Alexander Henry & Sons, Edinburgh, 1873, National Museums Scotland

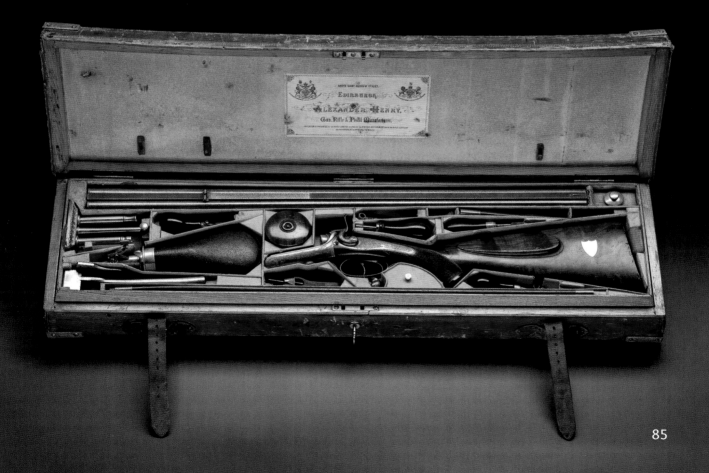

Imperial icons

During the Victorian period, the Highland regiments of the British army became ever more visible as representatives of Scotland's role in enforcing the power of the British Empire. In the 1850s their success in battles such as Balaklava in the Crimea and Lucknow in India were celebrated in imagery and print as part of the popular culture of imperialism.

Following the fashion, the army's Scottish Lowland regiments introduced tartan and other elements of Highland military dress into their uniforms. The status of military bagpiping was formally recognised, and military piping became the dominant standard in bagpipe performance and competition.

Military uniform had a strong influence on civilian Highland dress, encouraging uniformity in what was becoming a national costume for Scotland.

Above: Figurine of General Sir Colin Campbell

Sir Colin Campbell was a renowned Scottish soldier. Earthenware figures such as this were mass-produced in Staffordshire and sold to a public eager to celebrate and commemorate Britain's imperial victories.

*c.*1860, National Museums Scotland

Opposite: *74th Regiment of Foot*

This painting features Sir Eyre John Crabbe of the 74th Highlanders on horseback surrounded by his officers. It is a celebration of Crabbe's success in restoring tartan to the regiment in 1845.

By Daniel Cunliffe (1826–55), 1846, oil on canvas. On loan from Lunan Bay Hotel. Image © National Museums Scotland

Gaelic voices

Upholding rights

But I trust that it will not be long
Before this treachery will be put behind us,
That you won't see the eviction notice so often
Like a fiery cross throughout the country;
May the Queen stand on the side of the Gaels
As kindly Esther was on the side of the Jews,
And may every Haman who was oppressing us
Suffer resentment with an agonised heart.

Archibald Campbell,
***Song on the State of the Highlands*, 1851**

For the Perthshire poet Archibald Campbell, the young Queen Victoria's passion for the Highlands promised that she could be for Gaels like the Biblical Queen Esther was for the Jews. Just as Esther protected her people from Persian hostility, so Victoria could right the injustices of the Highland Clearances.

In Lowland towns and cities, middle-class Gaelic communities, often organised in societies based on clan or district origins, made much of the celebrated image of the heroic, loyal Highlander to lobby for the welfare of their fellow Gaels in the Highlands, as well as for cultural recognition and respect from the British state.

Guthan nan Gàidheal

A' seasamh chòraichean

Ach tha mi 'g earbsa air bheagan aimsir
Gun tèid a' chealgaireachd seo air chùl,
'S nach fhaic sibh bhàirlinn cho tric 's a bha i
Mar chrois-tàra air feadh na dùthch';
Gun seas a' Bhàn-righinn air taobh nan Gàidheal
Mar rinn Esther chàirdeil air taobh nan Iùdhach,
'S gum bi gach Hàman a bha gar sàrach'
Le cridhe cràiteach a' fulang diùmb.

Gilleasbaig Caimbeul,
***Òran air Cor na Gàidhealtachd**, 1851*

Bha Gilleasbaig Caimbeul, bàrd à Raineach, a' samhlachadh an trom-ghaoil a dh'fhairich Bànrigh Bhictòria òg don Ghàidhealtachd ris mar a bha a' Bhànrigh Ester sa Bhìoball do na h-Iùdhaich. Dìreach mar a dhìon Ester na daoine aice fhèin bho nàimhdeas nam Persianach, chuireadh Bhictòria ceart ana-ceartas nam Fuadaichean.

Ann am bailtean na Galldachd bhiodh bùirdeasaich às a' Ghàidhealtachd a' cur chomann air chois, glè thric ceangailte ri sloinnidhean no sgìrean sònraichte. Bhiodh iad a' dèanamh feum de dh'ìomhaigh a' Ghàidheil dhìlis ghaisgeil gus còraichean nan càirdean aca air ais aig an dachaigh a sheasamh, agus gus aithne agus spèis a bhuannachadh bho rìoghachd Bhreatainn.

Alexander Carmichael

The fokelorist Alexander Carmichael (1832–1912) was a significant figure in Gaelic scholarship during the late 19th and early 20th centuries. In 1900, Carmichael published his seminal work, the *Carmina Gadelica*. This was an assemblage of sacred pieces, hymns and charms based on Carmichael's collecting and research into Gaelic history, language and culture.

Tartan samples

These tartan swatches are from a collection of native textiles compiled by Alexander Carmichael during his travels in the Outer Hebrides in the late 19th century.

Late 18th and early 19th century, National Museums Scotland

John Francis Campbell of Islay

John Francis Campbell of Islay (1821–85) was
also influential. Known as Iain Òg Ìle, Young
John of Islay, he was heir to the island of Islay,
until his father was forced to sell his estate in
1847. Inspired by the ancestral tales and songs
related to him by his childhood nurse and the
family piper, Campbell set out to record the
traditional folklore of the Highlands and Islands.

With the assistance of contemporary
scholars, such as Hector MacLean, Hector
Urquhart, John Dewar and Alexander Carmichael,
Campbell amassed a vast collection of original
manuscripts related to Gaelic language and
literature, which was later published as *Popular
Tales of the West Highlands*.

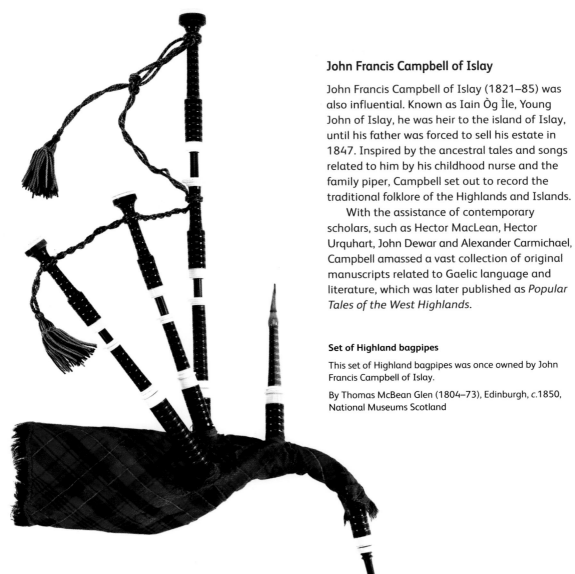

Set of Highland bagpipes

This set of Highland bagpipes was once owned by John
Francis Campbell of Islay.

By Thomas McBean Glen (1804–73), Edinburgh, *c*.1850,
National Museums Scotland

Celtic Revival

In the late 19th and early 20th centuries, there was a 'Celtic Revival'
in art, design and scholarship. The movement placed increased
emphasis on maintaining authenticity when drawing romantic
inspiration from the past. Spurred by new archaeological finds and
a fresh appreciation of pan-European Celtic art forms, the Celtic
Revival in Scotland moved beyond the standard popular image of
the Highlander. A number of Gaelic scholars brought serious and
systematic investigation to folklore studies during this period, including Alexander Carmichael (opposite) and John Francis Campbell
of Islay (above).

Legacy

The romantic ideas about Scotland that were first popularised during the 18th century are still with us today. While these ideas represent only a partial picture of this country's culture and history, they were not mere inventions. Behind the cultivation of this romantic image, there lay a genuine desire to preserve traditions that were seen to make Scotland unique.

The wild and majestic beauty of this country, and the sense of the past which it evokes, still fire our imaginations. Now, just as 200 years ago, Scotland's landscape, music, dress and history continue to be sources of pride and inspiration.

Acknowledgements

National Museums Scotland would like to thank the following sources for images and objects used in this book, and assistance with its publication:

An Comunn Gàidhealach and Lothian Gaelic Choir – page 92; Black Watch Castle and Museum – page 41; Blair Castle Collection – page 73; Bodleian Libraries, University of Oxford – page 61; British Museum – pages 27, 42–43; City of Edinburgh Council – pages 50–51; High Life Highland – pages 39, 81; Inverness Museum & Art Gallery – page 23; Lunan Bay Hotel – pages 86–87; MacDougall of Dunollie Preservation Trust – page 80; Museum of the Isles, Armadale Castle, Isle of Skye – page 55; National Galleries of Scotland – pages 8–9, 22, 30, 34–35, 40, 52, 54, 55, 58, 66–67, 77; National Library Scotland – page 24; National Museums Scotland – pages 1, 5, 6, 7, 10, 11, 13, 16, 17, 25, 26, 31, 36, 37, 38, 45, 46, 48, 49, 53, 58, 59, 64, 65, 67, 68, 69, 73, 74, 75, 76, 80, 81, 85, 86–87, 90, 91, 92; National Trust for Scotland – cover, page 29; Private Collections – pages 17, 31, 52; Reidhaven Trust – page 12; Rotherham Heritage Services – page 25; Royal Collection Trust – pages 4–5, 14–15, 20–21, 47, 78, 79, 82–83, 84; Salford Museum & Art Gallery – page 95; Scottish Tartans Authority – pages 36, 44, 49; University of Aberdeen – pages 70–71

Art Fund_

Page 59 – Acquired with the aid of the Art Fund

With grateful thanks to the curators, conservators, photographers, picture library and publishing staff, collections services, exhibition, design and administrative staff who have contributed to this book.

Opposite: *Ossian's Grave*

Macpherson's Ossian remained a source of inspiration for artists well into the 19th century. This scene of an ancient standing stone, meant to mark the final resting place of Ossian, was painted on the Isle of Arran.

By John MacWhirter (1839–1911), *c.*1882, oil on canvas, Salford Museum & Art Gallery

Further reading

Anderson, Caroline and Christopher Fleet 2018. *Scotland: Defending the Nation* (Edinburgh: Birlinn Limited).

Brown, Ian (ed) 2012. *From Tartan to Tartanry: Scottish Culture, History and Myth* (Edinburgh: Edinburgh University Press).

Brown, Iain Gordon (ed) 2003. *Abbotsford and Sir Walter Scott: The Image and the Influence* (Edinburgh: Society of Antiquaries of Scotland).

Cameron, Ewen 2010. *Impaled upon the Thistle: Scotland since 1880* (Edinburgh: Edinburgh University Press).

Cheape, Hugh 2006. *Tartan: The Highland Habit*, third edition (Edinburgh: NMS Enterprises Limited – Publishing).

Clyde, Robert 1995. *From Rebel to Hero: The Image of the Highlander 1745–1830* (East Linton: Tuckwell Press).

Devine, Sir Tom M 2018. *The Scottish Clearances: A History of the Dispossessed 1500–1900* (London: Allen Lane).

Dunbar, John Telfer 1962. *History of Highland Dress* (Glasgow: Glasgow University Press).

Durie, Alastair J 2012. *Travels in Scotland 1788–1881* (Suffolk: Boydell & Brewer for Scottish History Society).

Hunter, James 2016. *Set adrift upon the World: The Sutherland Clearances* (Edinburgh: Birlinn Limited).

Mackillop, Andrew 2000. *More Fruitful than the Soil: Army, Empire and the Scottish Highlands, 1715–1815* (East Linton: Tuckwell Press).

Macleod, Anne 2012. *From an Antique Land: Visual Representations of the Highlands and Islands 1700–1880* (Edinburgh: John Donald).

Miers, Mary 2017. *Highland Retreats: The Architecture and Interiors of Scotland's Romantic North* (New York: Rizzoli International).

Morton, Graeme 2012. *Ourselves and Others: Scotland, 1832–1914* (Edinburgh: Edinburgh University Press).

Pentland, Gordon 2011. *The Spirit of the Union: Popular Politics in Scotland, 1815–1820* (London: Pickering & Chatto).

Pittock, Murray 2009. *The Myth of the Jacobite Clans: The Jacobite Army in 1745*, second edition, (Edinburgh: Edinburgh University Press).

Stewart, Donald William (ed) 2008. *The Life and Legacy of Alexander Carmichael* (Ness: Islands Book Trust).

Trevor-Roper, Hugh 2009. *The Invention of Scotland: Myth and History* (New Haven and London: Yale University Press).